THE RESPONSIBILITY OF DISSENT:
THE CHURCH AND ACADEMIC FREEDOM

The
Responsibility of Dissent:
The Church and Academic Freedom

by JOHN F. HUNT
and TERRENCE R. CONNELLY
with CHARLES E. CURRAN, ROBERT E. HUNT
and ROBERT K. WEBB

A Search Book
Sheed and Ward: New York

© Sheed & Ward, Inc., 1969
Standard Book Number: 8362-0039-x (Paperback Edition)
and 8362-0122-1 (Library Edition)
Library of Congress Number: 73-92531

Manufactured in the U.S.A.

Acknowledgments

We are grateful for the opportunity which the law firm of Cravath, Swaine & Moore afforded to us to participate in this case and thus to extend the public service traditions of the Bar to contemporary university life.

We are grateful for the opportunity to collaborate with the subject professors and their distinguished academic counsel, Professor Robert K. Webb, of Columbia University and the *American Historical Review*.

We publicly express our appreciation to the members of the Inquiry Board and to the Board's counsel, Alfred L. Scanlan, Esq.

We are grateful to our distinguished expert witnesses:

Dr. John C. Bennett, President of Union Theological Seminary;

Professor Walter J. Burghardt, S.J., of Woodstock College, Editor of *Theological Studies* (and now a member of the Vatican International Commission of Theologians);

Dr. Robert D. Cross, President of Hunter College (and now President of Swarthmore College);

The Reverend Doctor Clarence W. Friedman, Associate Secretary, College and University Department, The National Catholic Educational Association;

The Reverend Theodore M. Hesburgh, C.S.C., President of the University of Notre Dame;

The Reverend John F. Hotchkin, of the Bishops' Committee for Ecumenism and Inter-Religious Affairs (National Conference of Catholic Bishops);

Professor Bernard J. F. Lonergan, S.J., of Regis College, Toronto, Canada;

Professor John T. Noonan, Jr., of the School of Law
(Boalt Hall) at the University of California, Berkeley;

Professor Gerard Sloyan, of the Department of Religion, Temple University;

Dean John H. Thirlkel, S.S., of the School of Theology,
St. Mary's University and Seminary;

Mr. Kenneth Woodward, Religion Editor of *Newsweek*
Magazine; and

The Reverend Victor R. Yanitelli, S.J., President of
Saint Peter's College.

Finally, we are grateful to the staff of the American Association
of University Professors in Washington, D.C. Its members gener-
ously afforded the benefit of their experience and expertise not only
to the administration of Catholic University but to us as counsel
for the subject professors and as novices in the field of academic
due process and academic freedom. As lawyers we would like to
make a special expression of gratitude to Mr. Herman I. Orent-
licher, Associate Secretary and Counsel of the Association.

The subject professors dedicate this volume to those who joined them in upholding the right of Catholic dissent from *Humanae Vitae*—especially those unjustly accused of disloyalty without benefit of due process.

The Professors Subject to Inquiry at Catholic University
William W. Bassett
John Cavanagh
Christian Ceroke
Charles E. Curran
Leo A. Foley, S.M.
George T. Dennis, S.J.
Robert E. Hunt
Thomas Joyce, C.M.F.
George A. Kanoti, C.R.
Peter J. Kearney
Daniel C. Maguire
Berard L. Marthaler
Alfred McBride, O. Praem.
Bernard J. McGinn
Roland E. Murphy, O. Carm.
Russell G. Ruffino
Warren Reich
John F. Smolko
Paul K. K. Tong
David W. Tracy

Academic Counsel to the Subject Professors
Robert K. Webb

Legal Counsel to the Subject Professors
John F. Hunt
Terrence R. Connelly

Preface

On July 30, 1968, a Statement by Catholic theologians, upholding a dissent from the Papal Encyclical *Humanae Vitae* (issued the day before) was released to the press in Washington, D.C. The idea of such a public Statement originated with some members of the faculty of The Catholic University of America and they were instrumental in organizing, drafting and publishing the Statement. In all, twenty-one * members of the University's faculty subscribed to the Statement. The Trustees of the University issued a press release on September 5, 1968, asserting that the foregoing public conduct raised "serious questions" under norms of responsible academic procedure, mandating an Inquiry to determine whether or not the professors had violated their various responsibilities to the University and as teachers of sacred sciences and threatening with suspension any subject professor who refused to refrain from any public comment inconsistent with pronouncements of the Church hierarchy.

After an exhaustive consideration of expert testimony, various exhibits, the written and oral testimony of the dissenting professors and the stipulation of facts agreed upon by the professors and the Trustees' representative to the Inquiry, a faculty Inquiry Board convened pursuant to the Trustees' mandate unanimously concluded on April 1, 1969, that the professors had acted responsibly in their dissent; that their Statement was tenable within the permissible spectrum of Catholic theology; and that the Trustees' threat of suspension had denied the professors academic due process.

* Various subsequent references count them as twenty since one subscribing teacher resigned from the University at the end of the fall semester.

The Trustees, after two months delay, accepted the Inquiry Report in so far as it related to the academic propriety of the dissenting professors' conduct, but did not acknowledge the Report's criticism of their own action. They also purported that they did not mean to express any approval of the theological position of the dissenters, although the Report they accepted had held the dissent to be "tenable" theologically.

As legal counsel for the professors subject to the Inquiry at Catholic University, we believe that the proceedings contributed significant materials bearing on current problems of the American institutions of higher education, particularly church-related schools. This book is intended to make those materials accessible to interested persons and to offer our conclusions as to their significance.

The Inquiry presented particular challenges to counsel. Many of the real issues in the case were obfuscated; many of those in the University with whom we dealt were unduly sensitive to the presence of attorneys; and most of the highly educated faculty Inquiry Board members were, like counsel, not familiar with the theological context of the dissent in question. Moreover, as the following account details, the professors ultimately had to assume the burden of proving themselves innocent of any professional irresponsibility.

The first part of the professors' case, which deals with the theological justification for their dissenting position and their manner of promulgating it, is set forth in the companion volume to this work entitled *Dissent In and For the Church: Theologians and Humanae Vitae.*

This work, which essentially is a case study of the Inquiry into the professors' dissent, sets forth the history of the Inquiry and publishes the documentary record of the prepared testimony which was presented on behalf of the professors with respect to the propriety of their actions under existing norms of academic responsibility. Several expert witnesses also testified in the Inquiry on behalf of the subject professors.

The factual data set forth are based primarily on materials of record in the Inquiry proceedings and otherwise based on materials

gathered by us in connection with our representation of the professors. We take full responsibility for their accuracy and for our
treatment of existing academic freedom and responsibility materials.
In particular, we take full responsibility for the opinions expressed
in the concluding chapter.

It seems to us appropriate to call attention to the significance of
this work as a case study of an investigation of dissent. In an effort
to preserve the form of the argument made to the Inquiry Board
on behalf of the professors, this work does not address itself to
any manifestation of dissent within or without the University context other than that engaged in by the subject professors. Nor
does this work by its description and defense of the professors'
mode of dissent purport to make any comment on the propriety
of other possible forms of dissent. The dissent at Catholic University is certainly at most an allegory in respect of the manifestation
of dissent now being experienced in many quarters of the American
academic community. Nonetheless, there are lessons in the case
respecting the "responsibility of dissent" for all those who would,
like the professors, engage in dissension and all those, like some
of the Catholic University Trustees, who would suppress it.

The theological controversy about the dissent at Catholic University shares certain problems that are common to all forms of
dissent in our society. There has been a persistent tension in our
culture between the ideal principle of freedom of expression and
the practical presumption that expressions of dissent provide a reasonable basis for questioning the loyalty of those who engage in it.
No detailed citation of history, remote or recent, is necessary to
show that the expression of dissent, though not punished by law,
has often been penalized by men who apply the cruel presumption
of disloyalty to those who disagree with the established order. In
the Roman Catholic Church today, "faith" and loyalty to inherited
institutional forms are being falsely equated to condemn those who
distinguish faith from such a loyalty. In our civil society, the concepts of "law" and "order," two distinct notions each with its own
set of relationships to other societal values, have become falsely
equated in the most popular slogans of the day.

In this context, the fight for academic freedom of expression at Catholic University has a distinct lesson for American society which must not go unmentioned. Even as it calls to mind the Church's commitment to truth and human dignity, it also calls to mind the precious nature of our society's commitment to freedom of expression, in the face of pressures to compromise that commitment. It reemphasizes the critical function of universities in society in the face of pressures to restrict the ambit of university involvement in contemporary problems. Moreover, it emphasizes the fact that freedom of expression does not truly exist in any society which presumes dissent to be guilty until it proves itself innocent.

John F. Hunt
Terrence R. Connelly

August 20, 1969

Contents

THE RESPONSIBILITY OF DISSENT: THE CHURCH AND ACADEMIC FREEDOM

1

The Dissent:
The Statement
by Catholic Theologians
of July 30, 1968

> *"As Roman Catholic theologians, conscious of our duty and our limitations, we conclude that spouses may responsibly decide according to their conscience that artificial contraception in some circumstances is permissible and indeed necessary to preserve and foster the values and sacredness of marriage."—Statement by Catholic Theologians, July 30, 1968, Washington, D. C.*

On July 29, 1968, Pope Paul VI issued an Encyclical entitled *Humanae Vitae* (of Human Life) in which he specifically taught that birth control by any method other than periodic abstinence (rhythm) was illicit. The text and context of the Encyclical indicated that, while the Pope was not purporting to teach "infallibly," he intended his teaching, which reiterated the 1930 pronouncement of Pope Pius XI's Encyclical *Casti Connubii*, to be binding without exception; he called on all other Roman Catholic teachers to support his teaching. Since the birth control debate had been raging in Roman Catholic circles for some years, it was clear that the Pope intended to terminate further debate by his "authoritative" teaching.

Rumors that such a papal action was forthcoming had been circulating since the spring. Indeed, five American bishops only one month before the Encyclical was released had issued instructional Guidelines for their respective jurisdictions (including Baltimore, Maryland, and Washington, D.C.), which proposed an absolutely binding teaching against any use of artificial contraception in marriage. Later the rumors were substantiated when *Time* magazine purchased from a Vatican source a copy of the text of the Encyclical a few days before its release on July 29.

On the afternoon of July 29, a group of ten Roman Catholic teachers of "sacred sciences" (using that term to include theology, philosophy, sacred Scripture, canon law and related specialties) procured several copies of the full text of the Encyclical released by the National Catholic News Service. These theologians met on the campus of The Catholic University of America in Washington, D.C., to analyze, discuss and evaluate the Encyclical. They recalled that common theological teaching in the Church allowed for dissent from noninfallible pronouncements of the Pope when sufficient reason to dissent existed. They had long been professionally familiar with the birth control issue and had been, of course, alert to the imminence of the papal pronouncement; two of them, in fact, had recently prepared professional commentaries on the aforementioned Guidelines. They found themselves in professional disagreement with the methodology of the Encyclical and, more importantly, concluded that notwithstanding the papal teaching husbands and wives might responsibly decide according to their consciences that artificial contraception "in some instances is permissible and indeed necessary to preserve and foster the values and sacredness of marriage." Moreover, aware that many other Roman Catholic theologians were in agreement (in the methodology of theology a measure of concurrence by peers having a substantive importance for the soundness of a position), they decided to frame and issue a public statement of their views on the Encyclical. Between 9 p.m. on July 29, when they had a draft public statement in hand, and 10:00 a.m. on July 30, eighty-seven Roman Catholic theologians from twenty-four different colleges, universities and theologates concurred (many via telephone) in the proposed statement and had agreed to be publicly identified

as subscribers to it. At 10:00 a.m. on July 30, the Statement by
Catholic Theologians (see Appendix A), together with the names
and institutional identifications of the then eighty-seven subscribers,
was released to the press and thereupon received wide national
publicity on radio and television. This *immediate, organized public
dissent* by Roman Catholic scholars from a formal and authoritative papal teaching was unprecedented in Church history.

Twelve of the original subscribers, including a majority of the
original draftsmen, were members of the regular faculty (as distinguished from the summer school faculty) of The Catholic University of America. The draftsmen from Catholic University were
Charles E. Curran, Robert E. Hunt, Daniel C. Maguire, Alfred
McBride and Russell G. Ruffino, all clerics. In addition, the
original subscribers included the following regular faculty members from Catholic University: William W. Bassett, Christian
Ceroke, George A. Kanoti, Peter J. Kearney, Berard L. Marthaler,
Bernard J. McGinn and David W. Tracy (also all clerics). The
later subscribers from the regular faculty at Catholic University
were George T. Dennis, Leo A. Foley, Thomas Joyce, Roland E.
Murphy, Warren Reich, John Smolko and Paul K. K. Tong (all
clerics). John Cavanagh, M.D., a Lecturer at the University's
School of Theology also later subscribed to the Statement. Although eventually more than 600 theologians from over 200 colleges and universities subscribed to the Statement, and although
there were other subsequent statements of dissent, the controversy
which the Theologians' Statement kindled focused at Catholic
University. The University is a unique institution in the United
States by virtue of the fact that it is sponsored by all the American
bishops and has the status of a "pontifical" university. In the face
of this, members of its faculty had led the dissent in the United
States.

The joint publication of the Statement of dissent from *Humanae
Vitae,* was, of course, inconsistent with the view, not uncommon
in some Catholic circles, that the role of the theological scholar in
the Church was to offer his supporting services to the pronouncements of the hierarchical teaching office of the Church, or else to

be silent. Moreover, those who held this view, which included many members of the American hierarchy, considered the Statement to be a scandalous, disloyal action. Such challenges raised a central question: can a Roman Catholic dissent from an authoritative papal teaching and still claim good standing with the Catholic Church? The Statement, of course, had insisted that such a right to dissent existed in the Church and was applicable to the birth control Encyclical. The Statement inherently also claimed that those who did so dissent had the right to make their views public.

While these issues are essentially Catholic *intellectual* issues, they were joined in a practical context. The Statement, by communicating the right to dissent, told millions of troubled Catholics that their apparent choice between their own consciences and the papal teaching on contraception was a false dilemma: the theologians asserted that Catholics could dissent in practice on the issue *without* putting themselves outside the Church. Many troubled bishops, however, felt that the dissenting theologians were going beyond the bounds of their science and usurping a pastoral teaching function that properly belonged solely to the hierarchy. The Statement by Catholic Theologians, therefore, was not only a continuation of the birth control controversy but also a springboard to new questions on the right to dissent itself and on the role and relationship of bishops and theologians. These questions gradually focused at the University where the public Statement of dissent originated.

The day before the Theologians' Statement was promulgated, Patrick Cardinal O'Boyle of Washington had issued a statement on the binding force of the Encyclical. O'Boyle called for absolute obedience to the Encyclical "without equivocation, ambiguity or simulation." The Chairman of the National Conference of Catholic Bishops, Archbishop John Dearden of Detroit, polled his fellow bishops on the day of the Theologians' Statement and on the next day issued a statement calling on Catholics to "receive [the Encyclical] with sincerity . . . to study it carefully, and to form their consciences in its light."[1] Robert Springer, S.J., Professor of Moral Theology from Woodstock College, and Professor Curran, two of the draftsmen of the Theologians' Statement, immediately suggested that the bishops (albeit indirectly) had left room for responsible dissent from the Encyclical. However, a spokesman for the bishops responded that the bishops in no way intended "to imply that there is any difference between their statement and the teaching of the Holy Father."[2] The American bishops, as a group, then fell silent for the time being. Individual bishops, however, particularly prominent members of the hierarchy, launched a series of direct attacks on the dissenting theologians. Most prominent of such attacks were those of Cardinal O'Boyle.

Cardinal O'Boyle had become involved in a dispute with some of his diocesan clergy who had issued a statement of conscience declaring that in their pastoral work (such as hearing confessions) they would respect responsibly formed dissenting consciences with respect to the Encyclical. Cardinal O'Boyle was to take the position that, as a bishop, he could give pastoral faculties only to clerics who would exercise them consistent with the teachings of the Church, and that acknowledging the possibility of licit dissent from *Humanae Vitae* was not consistent with the teachings of the Church. The members of his diocesan clergy who disagreed cited the Statement by Catholic Theologians for support: if the theologians were right in asserting that dissent on the issue of birth control was permissible within the framework of Catholic teaching, then the Cardinal's position was impeached. By virtue of its pontifical charter, the Cardinal was also the Chancellor of Catholic University.

Other leading members of the American hierarchy made statements highly critical of the dissenting theologians.[3] Cardinal O'Boyle set the theme: the dissenters were "setting the Church on fire."[4] Others included Archbishop Robert E. Lucey of San Antonio, who declared in a letter to his Archdiocese:

. . . These arguments (of the dissenting theologians) are specious. In Texas we call them hogwash. . . .
When the Holy Father recently confirmed the traditional teaching of the Church about artificial birth control . . . some little theologians —Catholic and non-Catholic; laymen and even ladies—rushed pell-

mell into battle with colors flying and arms waving to condemn the decision of the Supreme Pontiff. . . .[5]

In another pastoral letter, Bishop Albert L. Fletcher of Little Rock defended the Encyclical and deplored the "dissent and disagreement from many so-called Catholic experts. . . . One is inclined to wonder if these men have much faith and the humility that goes with it."[6] Bishop John Wright of Pittsburgh offered a popular analogy to justify such criticism of the dissenters:

. . . Given the acclaim some of the experts opposing the Holy Father presently command and the unpopularity he well knew his authoritative decision would provoke, world reaction to the Pope's bold, historic action recalls the excitement all over the United States the night of President Truman's plucky firing of Douglas MacArthur.

The parallel is imperfect, of course; the Church is not literally an army and the setting forth of religious truth is not the same as the development of political or military tactic. However, the parallel is, in its way, instructive. The professionals have been fully consulted and patiently heard; the leader has finally spoken as only he could and should do.

It now remains to be seen whether lesser spokesmen among the people of God have a sense of responsibility and order proportionate to that of the subordinate chieftains of the wisdom of the world. General MacArthur acted with great grace in response to his commander-in-chief and in accordance with the pledged word which constituted him in his proper place and dignity. . . .[7]

Bishop Wright had been the principal author of the most recent statement of the National Conference of Catholic Bishops touching on the question of the teaching authority of the Church hierarchy. That statement, the 1967 Pastoral Letter, *The Church in Our Day,* had not adequately distinguished between infallible and noninfallible hierarchical pronouncements, between matters of *faith* and other matters, in outlining the assent owed by Catholics to Church teachings. Two Catholic University faculty members who were to be among the subscribers to the Theologians' Statement (Professors Tracy and Hunt) had informed one of the bishop consultants to the drafting committee for the 1967 Pastoral of

those inadequacies, but no changes were made in the final
version. If the dissenting theologians were correct in asserting that
dissent from the Encyclical was a Catholic possibility, the American
bishops had failed to give adequate pastoral directive to American
Catholics.

Meanwhile, despite the bishops' pronouncements, scholarly support for the Theologians' Statement multiplied in quantity and
quality. A copy of the Statement was mailed on behalf of the 87
original subscribers by John F. Cronin, S.S., Professor of Moral
Theology at St. Mary's University and Seminary (Baltimore),
Edwin F. Falteisek, S.J., Head of the Department of Pastoral Theology at the School of Divinity, St. Louis University, and Professor
Curran to approximately 1,200 members of the Catholic Theological Society of America and the College Theology Society, together
with a letter inviting those addressees who wished to become subscribers to return the enclosed postcard marked to that effect (this
mailing produced the more than 600 professional affirmations of
the Statement; 52 negative replies were received). At a press conference on August 1, all the lay members from the United States
of the Papal Birth Control Commission also announced their agreement with the Statement in accordance with their respective com-
petencies. (The Commission had been appointed by Pope Paul to
study the birth control question, and a majority of its members
concluded in favor of revision of the Church's absolute prohibition of artificial contraception.) These subscribers included Dr.
John R. Cavanagh, a Washington psychiatrist and Visiting Lecturer
in Pastoral Psychology at Catholic University, Professor John T.
Noonan, Jr., of the School of Law at the University of California,
Berkeley, (the special consultant on history to the papal commission), together with Professors André Hellegers and Thomas K.
Burch of Georgetown University, Professor Donald Barrett of
Notre Dame and Mr. and Mrs. Patrick Crowley of Chicago, Illinois. After the July 30 and August 1 press conferences, subscribers
to the Theologians' Statement received many invitations to speak
with journalists from the press, radio and television. While most of
these invitations were refused, a few were accepted to provide neces-

sary background for the Statement. For example, on August 1, the CBS radio network broadcast a taped discussion between Professor Curran and Professor Austin Vaughan of St. Joseph's Seminary of the Archdiocese of New York, who challenged the legitimacy of the Theologians' Statement in terms of Catholic theology. (In this interview, as in the other press encounters, the dissenters did not take any positions beyond the substance of the Theologians' Statement itself.) By mid-August, as a result of overwhelming scholarly support coupled with wide dissemination through the mass media, the Statement had made broad and permanent impact. It had by then become clear that the Encyclical would not be received as the final word of the Roman Catholic Church on the problem of birth control.

The Catholic University professors were a specific target of much of the criticism that accompanied the publication of the Theologians' Statement. Editorial opinion in some Catholic newspapers and periodicals had been severely critical of the dissenting theologians, especially those at Catholic University. If dissent from the Encyclical was disloyal, dissent at Catholic University was treason. And the guardian of orthodoxy at the University, under its Vatican "charter" or Statutes, was the Chancellor, Cardinal O'Boyle, who from the beginning denied the possibility of licit dissent from the Encyclical.[8] In this context, the Acting Rector of the University, the Reverend John P. Whalen, organized a meeting among some of the dissenters and those who challenged their dissent. The meeting was intended as a discussion of the pastoral effects and implications of the Encyclical and the dissent from it.

There were fourteen participants at the meeting, held at the Statler-Hilton Hotel in New York on August 18 and 19. Seven who had dissented from the Encyclical attended: three Catholic University theologians—Professors Curran, Hunt, and Maguire—as well as Professor Walter Burghardt, S.J., of Woodstock College; Bernard Haering, C.SS.R., a German teaching at the Academia Alfonsiana in Rome; Professor James Megivern, C.M., of St. John's University; and Professor John T. Noonan, Jr. Three theologians who took issue with the dissent in varying degrees attended:

Reverend Paul McKeever, editor, Long Island Catholic; Professor Carl Peter of Catholic University, and Professor Austin Vaughan of St. Joseph's Seminary, Yonkers, New York. Four American bishops were present: Bishop Joseph Bernardin, General Secretary of the National Conference of Catholic Bishops; Archbishop Philip Hannan of New Orleans, a Trustee of the University; Bishop John Wright of Pittsburgh, who did not attend the session on Monday, August 19; and Bishop Alexander Zaleski of Lansing, a Trustee of the University and Chairman of the American Bishops' Committee on Doctrine. (Cardinal O'Boyle declined an invitation to attend.)

The discussions at the meeting focused to some extent on the question of the *right* to dissent from authoritative and noninfallible papal pronouncements. The professors present who had subscribed to the Statement presented scholarly statements demonstrating the roots of their position in the traditional teaching of the Church, including evidence that even the "manualist" school of theological authors of the late nineteenth and early twentieth centuries (characterized by a generally conservative pedagogical approach) indicated the distinct possibility of dissent as at times necessary and proper in the Church.

The discussion at the Statler-Hilton also focused, however, on the dissenters' *method* of promulgating their position—the so-called "manner and mode" issue. Briefly stated, the "manner and mode" objections raised by bishops and others at the Statler-Hilton meeting prescind from the question of whether dissent itself is permissible and focus rather on the group action in promulgating the dissent as a serious threat to the teaching function of bishops in the Church. Moreover, the "manner and mode" issue has from time to time been closely linked with allegations concerning the personal motivations of the dissenters, seeking to discredit the Statement as at best an imprudent resort to "secular" publicity or, worse, as a form of "conspiracy" to accomplish an evil purpose, usually described as "confusing the faithful". At the Statler-Hilton meeting, the dissenters pointed out the American bishops' failure in the 1967 Pastoral to distinguish the assent of divine faith from the conditional response known as "religious assent" and to articulate the possibility of Catholic dissent from noninfallible papal pronouncements, and maintained that consequently the exercise of the existing right to dissent by a group of theologians publicly was bound to be "confusing" to some. Furthermore, the dissenters pointed out that given the existence of the right to dissent within the Catholic faith, Catholics concerned with the issue involved had a "right to know" (recognized by the Second Vatican Council) about that right to dissent. Any temporary confusion, therefore, was at worst a necessary evil.

At this point of the discussions, an intervention occurred which was to re-emerge later in the course of the coming proceedings at Catholic University. Bishop Wright asked whether the dissenters admitted that they had knowingly produced confusion among the faithful: Professor Curran replied in the affirmative; then Bishop Wright declared his gratitude for the dissenters' frank admission that they were *purposely trying to confuse the faithful.* He directed his remarks at Professor Curran in particular. Other dissenters who were present quickly recalled the context of the discussion of "confusion"; that confusion was not the aim but an unfortunate and foreseeable by-product. Bishop Wright did not explore the problem further and did not return for the next day's sessions. But the charge that the professors were purposely trying to confuse the faithful was to surface again and, when reiterated, was to be directed to Professor Hunt, in particular, not Professor Curran.

The meeting at the Statler-Hilton ended on August 19 with agreement only on the proposition that further dialogue would be useful and perhaps necessary. However, ensuing developments foreclosed the possibilities for further dialogue.

Acting in his capacity as Chancellor of Catholic University, Cardinal O'Boyle (via a special delivery letter over signature of the Acting Rector) summoned the faculty of the School of Theology, the Department of Religious Education, and in particular, members of the Catholic University faculty who had signed the Theologians' Statement to a meeting at the University on August 20.

The Cardinal was concerned about the basic question of the right of dissent, not the "manner and mode" issue raised at the Statler-Hilton meeting. The latter question was not discussed at the Chancellor's meeting at all. The only question discussed was whether or not the right of dissent cited in the Statement by Catholic Theologians in fact existed as a common teaching in the Church. Chancellor O'Boyle had retained the services of two professors from outside Catholic University as theological advisors, Professors Germain Grisez and John Ford of Georgetown University and Weston (Massachusetts) College, respectively (both of whom objected to the dissent). The Chancellor, however, did not call the meeting to lay down an ultimatum. In this connection, it seems relevant to recall the so-called "Curran Affair" at Catholic University.

In the spring of 1967, the Trustees of the University had, upon five minutes' discussion, voted to intrude into the regular University processes and not allow Professor Curran's teaching contract to be renewed for the following academic year. He had already been unanimously recommended for promotion to the rank of Associate Professor by his Dean and faculty, and unanimously approved for continuance and promotion by the Academic Senate of the University. Normally, under Article 55 of the University Statutes, the Trustees have no part in the appointment or promotion of Associate Professors; such action is taken by the Rector, with consultation of the faculty or Department and of the Academic Senate. On April 17, 1967, the Rector, Bishop William McDonald, informed Professor Curran of the Trustees' nonrenewal mandate (in effect, a summary dismissal), avowed that he was only "following orders," and that no charges had been made and no reasons had been given. (Reportedly, Professor Curran's orthodoxy had been challenged under secret adjudicatory procedures provided in Article 66 of the University Statutes.[9] However, no charges, reasons, allegations or questions concerning his conduct or teaching have ever been given by the Rector or the Trustees.) The Trustees' action brought on an immediate, total faculty and student boycott, effectively closing down the entire University.

Professor Curran's basic human and academic rights had been violated and the professional judgment of the Dean and faculty of the School of Theology had been repudiated by the Trustees. Moreover, the entire community, faculty and students alike, realized that their own integrity as a University had suffered, and they affirmed that they would not and could not function "unless and until Professor Curran is reinstated." On what proved to be the last day of the one-week strike, after three hours of tense discussion, Chancellor O'Boyle emerged to read a statement "abrogating" the Trustees' action and Rector McDonald announced that Professor Curran would be issued a standard three-year contract as Associate Professor of Theology—a contract that brought with it permanent tenure at the University. Cardinal O'Boyle read the statement from the steps of Mullen Library to over 4,000 assembled students and faculty members and before the correspondents of all major newspaper, radio and television media in the United States.[10]

In August, 1968, the memories of the Curran affair lingered; furthermore, now it was not the conduct or teaching of *one* man that was in question, but the pronouncements of a score of the Catholic University faculty, joined by a growing list of their professional colleagues. Cardinal O'Boyle proceeded with caution.

At the meeting Chancellor O'Boyle was attended by the University's civil lawyers, a canon lawyer and a court reporter. After verifying the accuracy of the published list of subscribers to the Theologians' Statement from the Catholic University faculty, the Cardinal informed all present that he was acting in his capacity as Chancellor and asked the faculty members present to comment in regard to "the problems you think the (Theologians' Statement) might raise for us as a University."[11]

The testimony of Professor Carl Peter, a theologian who expressed some disagreement with the Theologians' Statement, was perhaps the most significant; despite his disagreement, and with an insight that was not to be appreciated until later, he said:

I concede, as I did long before the day arose, the right for responsible dissent, even to a Papal document.

The authors that Father Curran cited are *auctores probati*. Professor

Curran's citations were Catholic Theology. It was not popularly known. *We do have a problem in terms, I suppose, to finance . . . the university. If you ask me, I think there is a problem; it is not my business to worry about supporting the University.* I think there is going to be somewhat of a problem.

We can look at this as academic men, and I can see the right to responsible dissent even to a Papal decision which is not infallible; yes, to me . . . there is no question of this.

Now, where do we go from here? My conclusion is this; we have got to live with it. What would be more to be expected in the university than responsible dissent within the faith, within the realms of the Catholic Faith. I do not question, I have never questioned, the faith of my colleagues, of their allegiance to the Roman Pontiff. If I thought otherwise, I think I would say so within this group, but I do not. (Emphasis supplied.)

The dissenting professors likewise asserted that the Statement was a responsible, loyal Catholic expression. They cited the historical context of the Second Vatican Council's Constitution on the Church, particularly paragraph 25 calling for religious assent of mind and will with respect to papal teachings such as the Encyclical: the official response of the Council to proposed revisions (*Modus* 159) of that paragraph had acknowledged that paragraph 25 itself left room for the possibility of dissent from such teaching. As Professor Peter's testimony shows, they also referred the Cardinal to "approved authors," referred to by Vatican Council II, such as Dieckmann, Lercher, Palmieri, Straub, Pesch, Hervé, Van Noort and Karrer, who acknowledged, directly or indirectly, the possibility of licit dissent; Professor Curran read portions of the works of the "manualists" Pesch and Lercher into the record to substantiate their position.

No one rose to challenge the professors' right to dissent. Those who professionally disagreed with the particular dissent in question, such as Professor Peter, upheld its intellectual supportability within the Catholic faith. Jordan Kurland, Associate Secretary with the Washington Office of the American Association of University Professors (AAUP), who was present at the request of the dissenters, made clear that the Statement did not transgress AAUP's norm

for faculty conduct requiring professors not to create a false impression that they are university spokesmen:

Obviously, the signatories all have identities, but I don't think there is any argument that they were speaking in an official university capacity.

Thus the uncontradicted opinions of those present were that no real issues of academic propriety or religious loyalty were raised by the dissent and that the only problem was a problem of "finance." The Chancellor, however, near the end of the meeting, expressed a somewhat contrary view:

So I will simply say that many members of the faculty, and I am referring of course to the School of Theology, and the Department of Religious Education, and one member from the School of Philosophy, have expressed themselves here this morning, and I think the questions raised are so important and so complicated that it is very clear to me I will have to take the matter under advisement.

I certainly didn't come here with the thought of, as one newspaper expressed it, that this would be the "showdown".

Frankly, I believe I will have to refer the matter to the Board of Trustees and ask for a special meeting of the Board.

However, I would say this to you, that you can be of further valuable help to me if each of you individually would send me, as soon as you can, your own professional opinion—when I say "professional" I mean as Theologians, and professors and teachers in various schools —on two paragraphs of the statement.

They are the two paragraphs near the end, the one beginning with the words—and I quote—"It is common teaching in the Church. . . ." And also the one just after that.

These are on page 3 of the document which you received. The paragraph that reads, "It is common teaching in the Church that Catholics may dissent from authoritative, noninfallible teachings of the magisterium when sufficient reasons for so doing exist."

And then the next paragraph, "Therefore, as Roman Catholic theologians, conscious of our duty and our limitations, we conclude that spouses may responsibly decide according to their conscience that artificial contraception in some circumstances is permissible and indeed necessary to preserve and foster the values and sacredness of marriage."

The dissenters sought to discover the purpose of the Chancellor's course of action.

PROFESSOR HUNT: Another question I would have is if we are to give as theologians a rationale, or reckoning, and the reasons for concurring or nonconcurring, or reservations, or the acceptance of these two paragraphs, to whom should they be addressed, in the sense of what purpose would it serve? The only persons that could evaluate this theological exposition would be a peer group, namely theologians, and if that is right, what purpose would you intend?

CHANCELLOR O'BOYLE: I will tell you frankly. According to the statutes, there would have to be appointed, I think the statutes say three Bishops—is that correct?

[The Chancellor was referring to Article 66 of the papal Statutes, which authorizes a panel of three bishops to determine faculty offenses against Catholic doctrine.]

PROFESSOR HUNT: For what?

CHANCELLOR O'BOYLE: To meet with the members of the faculty.

PROFESSOR HUNT: I don't understand. For what purpose?

CHANCELLOR O'BOYLE: Let me get the book. Well, I can't lay my hands upon it, but I know the other day I saw it.

PROFESSOR CURRAN: I don't think, Your Eminence, that Article 66 justifies that type action.

CHANCELLOR O'BOYLE: Well, you may be right about Article 66, because we are not making any charges at the moment, one way or the other.

The dissenters noted for the record that the meeting in no way constituted a formal hearing, challenged the Chancellor's right to demand written responses even under Article 66 and obtained the Cardinal's agreement that voluntary written explanatory comments concerning the asserted right of dissent (either by individuals or a group) *received before October 1* would be acceptable.

The Chancellor had come to the meeting with a prepared press release. Near the end of the meeting he distributed his release and asked for comments. The dissenting professors pointed out that the press release was his and not theirs although they were willing to make their comments on the Chancellor's release. In "off the record" remarks the Chancellor indicated his intention of releasing the press statement and of making no further comments to the press. The professors, however, were to be free to talk to the press. Some of the dissenting professors answered questions posed by reporters waiting to see them at the conclusion of the meeting (although the professors had not alerted the press to the meeting). In these interviews, the professors played down any threat of discipline in the meeting and summarized the evidence they had presented to the Cardinal in support of their right to dissent.

On the morning of August 21 the Chancellor called acting Rector Whalen and the Dean of the School of Theology to his chancery office. He was quite irate both about the meeting and the subsequent publicity. The next day the Chancellor issued a five-page press release accusing by name two of the dissenters of "confusing the faithful" and of misrepresenting him, and implicitly criticizing the dissenters for speaking to the press, as if some agreement had been made that they would not. He charged that "two of the dissenting theologians, Rev. Charles Curran and Rev. Robert Hunt, immediately presented to the news media an account of the meeting that seriously misrepresented [Cardinal O'Boyle's] position." The Chancellor continued: "The false and misleading reports of the meeting suggested that my effort to be fair implied a vindication of the claimed 'right of dissent'. . . . Listening with patience does not imply agreement."[12]

Witnesses in the Inquiry that was to follow affirmed that the Cardinal explicitly said he had no objection if the professors wanted to talk to the press.

MR. SCANLAN (Counsel to the Faculty Board of Inquiry): At any time did he suggest that the press release which he had circulated and which he had previously prepared was to be the official version of the meeting?

THE WITNESS (Prof. Leo Farley, who was not a subscriber to the

Theologians' Statement): No, and in fact off the record he seemed to be making a point that he was not dictating in this area, that we were free to fashion our own press release; we were free to be interviewed or not to be interviewed, that this was his own personal determination in terms of himself alone.

MR. JOHN F. HUNT (Counsel to the professors subject to the Inquiry): Do you recall the meeting going off the record and do you recall what was said during that off-the-record interval?

THE WITNESS (DEAN WALTER SCHMITZ of the School of Theology): I did not know that it went off the record until I saw the copy myself. But I recall very distinctly what he said because I was the one that urged him at the end of the meeting that the press was outside, and we should make some sort of a statement.

After that statement had been agreed upon, then he did say as we walked out of the room—he said, "I don't intend to speak to these men. If any of the rest of you men want to speak with them, that is all right with me." [13]

None of the press stories concerning the meeting, either expressly by quotes, or by implication, showed the dissenters claiming that the fact of their meeting with the Chancellor had somehow vindicated their dissenting position. The dissenters had pointed out that they had presented evidence of their position which they felt vindicated them, but they in no way attempted to characterize Cardinal O'Boyle's frame of mind and in no way suggested that his patient listening was of itself a "vindication" of their substantive position on dissent. An unpublished press story on the wire of the National Catholic News Service had stated (without quotations) that Professor Curran felt vindicated by the meeting. However, the "vindicated" phrase was the newswriter's own summary conclusion, based on the fact that Professor Curran saw no further discipline in the meeting, and based on the data which Professor Curran presented in support of the common teaching in the Church on the right of dissent. [14] On August 22 the Chancellor called the reporter of the news service story and asked him whether Professor Curran actually had used the word "vindicated" to describe the meeting. The reporter told the Chancellor that he had not, and the news service story was "killed." Simultaneously, the Chancellor issued his press release charging the professors with claiming vindication. The Chancellor then commissioned an analysis by one of his consultants, Professor Germain Grisez, of the citations from the theology manuals that Professor Curran presented at the August 20 meeting, and proceeded to request a special meeting of the Trustees of the University.

Professor Leo Farley, a member of the Theology faculty who did not subscribe to the Statement and who attended the Chancellor's meeting, made public the following statement on August 24:

I must take exception to the chancellor's account and interpretation of the Tuesday (Aug. 20) meeting. Cardinal O'Boyle stated that the dissenting theologians "offered no evidence that the Catholic Church ever tolerated dissent of the sort they are carrying on and even instigating."

The stenotyped record shows that ample documentation drawn from standard and approved pre-Vatican II manuals of Catholic theology was presented as a vindication of the right and the responsibility of the dissenting theologians.

Previously on Sunday and Monday, August 18 and 19, at a New York meeting involving both theologians and Bishops, more ample documentation had already been supplied. The chancellor was invited to consult the minutes of this meeting.

Furthermore, "the dissenting theologians" offered a full bibliography and an opportunity to the chancellor for further discussion of the documentation. At this point it was the chancellor, rather than the theologians, who betrayed reluctance.

The chancellor in his statement questioned the competence of my confreres in that they did not have the results of their study ready at hand. We received the invitation fully a week prior to the meeting, yet without the slightest hint of the purpose of the meeting. An agenda was offered only after the doors were closed. Finally, all participants agreed on the formula, "as soon as possible," as an adequate expression of the willingness of the theologians to respond to the chancellor's request.[15]

Meanwhile, the dissenting professors for their part expressed astonishment at Cardinal O'Boyle's August 22 press release, maintaining that it was the Chancellor who was misrepresenting them, not they the Chancellor.

Notes

1. National Catholic News Service (Domestic), August 1, 1968.
2. *The Washington Post,* August 6, 1968, § B, p. 5.
3. See, e.g., Statement of Cardinal Krol (A Trustee of Catholic University), National Catholic News Service (Domestic), July 30, 1968.
4. Letter dated August 2, 1968, from Patrick Cardinal O'Boyle addressed to the Archdiocese of Washington.
5. United States Catholic Conference Documentary Service, August, 9, 1968.
6. National Catholic News Service (Domestic), August 6, 1968.
7. U.S. Catholic Conference Documentary Service, August 2, 1968.
8. Article 21, The Statutes of The Catholic University of America (1937, as amended, 1967).
9. G. Grisez, "Academic Freedom and Catholic Faith," *NCEA Bulletin* 15, 19 (November, 1967).
10. See generally A. Pierce, *Beyond One Man: Catholic University, April 17–24, 1967* (1967).
11. Transcript of the meeting with Chancellor of Catholic University and a number of members of the faculty of the School of Sacred Theology, the Department of Religious Education and the School of Philosophy (August 20, 1968); all quotations herein from the Chancellor's meeting of August 20 are taken from this Transcript, a copy of which is on file in the archives of Catholic University.
12. United States Catholic Conference Documentary Service, August 22, 1968.
13. Transcript of the Proceedings of the Faculty Board of Inquiry into the Statement of Dissent from the Encyclical *Humanae Vitae* by Professors at The Catholic University of America (January—March, 1969); further quotations from testimony offered to the Faculty Board of Inquiry are taken from this Transcript, which is on file in the Archives of The Catholic University.
14. National Catholic News Service (Domestic), August 21, 1968 (withdrawn the following day). See also *The Washington Post,* August 24, 1968, § D, p. 11.

15. National Catholic News Service (Domestic), August 26, 1968. The sense of the Transcript of the August 20 meeting is that all agreed that the theologians would furnish the Chancellor in writing the detailed scholarly support for their Statement as soon as possible but not later than October 1.

2

The Trustees' Reaction:
A Mandate for an Inquiry,
a Threat of Suspension
and a Call for Silence

"The Board directs the acting-Rector of the University to institute through due academic process an immediate inquiry as to whether the teachers at this University who signed the recent statement of dissent have violated by their declarations or their actions their responsibilities to the University. . . ."—Statement Concerning Dissenting Theologians at Catholic University, Board of Trustees of the Catholic University of America, September 5, 1968.

Twenty-nine of thirty Catholic University Trustees arrived in Washington for their special meeting of September 5 to consider the birth control dissent on the faculty. Three members of the Catholic University faculty attended as recently designated faculty representatives to the Trustees' meetings, with a voice but no vote. Bishop John Wright of Pittsburgh attended by invitation of the Board; none of the dissenting professors was invited. The Trustees were divided on the question of dissent into three distinct groups. One group, led by prominent members of the American hierarchy, considered that the dissent of the University was intolerable in view of its pontifical character, maintained that dissent was outside the pale of the Catholic confessional commitment and sought to separate the dissenters from the University. This point of view

23

was best exemplified by Cardinal McIntyre's lengthy motion, made early in the meeting, calling on the Board to declare that the dissenters, by subscribing to the Statement, had broken their profession of faith as faculty members and had, as a consequence, "resigned" as members of the faculty.

Other Trustees were sensitive to the University's recent affirmation of the principles of academic freedom. Barely a month earlier, the Trustees had promulgated a Statement of Objectives affirming that at Catholic University the "only constraint upon truth is truth itself." The opinion of these Trustees was that no special meeting (or special action) was then warranted.

A third group of Trustees might be called by many names: moderates, pragmatists, compromisers. They sought to achieve unanimity of the Board by arranging some acquiescence to the key demands of the opposing groups of Trustees: on the one hand, the silencing of the dissent and, on the other hand, an attempt to protect the reputation of the University in academic circles. Bishop James P. Shannon reflected the context of the Trustees' September 5 meeting in the following testimony given by him in his capacity as representative of the Board of Trustees during the Inquiry that was to follow:

> The meeting of the Board of Trustees in September . . . was taking place in a climate of opinion in which the Board was not certain what answers it should make to different constituencies that the Board must be concerned about, the public, the bishops, the academic community generally.

The basic fact the Trustees had before them was the Statement of dissent. Bishops Zaleski and Wright and Acting Rector Whalen also gave the Trustees their opinions concerning the Statler-Hilton meeting. Bishop Wright reported that the dissenters' attitude was at variance with Vatican II. Bishop Wright, however, said he thought the meeting was a good idea. Bishop Zaleski reported that the dissenters evidenced tendencies going beyond Vatican I and II involving a new concept of the role of the Pope, de-emphasizing his authority and stressing the consensus of the faithful. Acting

Rector Whalen was disappointed because the meeting did not remain on the "pastoral" level which he had intended. The dissenters had had no idea that their "attitude" at the Statler-Hilton meeting was under Trustee scrutiny in the context of possible disciplinary action; rather, they had understood the meeting as an effort at dialogue.

Cardinal O'Boyle repeated to the Trustees the allegations in his August 22 press release that two of the dissenting professors had misrepresented him by claiming "vindication" by his meeting of August 20, and again suggested that it was improper for the professors to have spoken to the press after the meeting. In addition, he specifically cited quotations, purportedly of Professors Curran and Hunt, stating that they "felt vindicated" and that their "right of dissent had been approved" by the August 20 meeting. Cardinal O'Boyle told the Trustees that these quotes appeared in *The Washington Post, The Washington Star* and *The Baltimore Sun.* The Trustees did not ask Cardinal O'Boyle to produce these newspaper quotations. The quotes were in fact utter and complete fabrications.

After these presentations, the Trustees focused their work that day on drafting a press release, which was to assert that the dissenters' conduct had "raised serious questions" in terms of responsible academic procedure. Bishop Shannon testified in the following manner when asked during the Inquiry to explain the source of those "serious questions":

MR. HUNT: I would like to know who put to the trustees, on or before September 5, questions as to the propriety, in accordance with accepted academic standards, of our actions in connection with the encyclical.

BISHOP SHANNON: I would be glad to speak to that.

I don't know, Mr. Hunt. I am sure I can't give you a complete answer to that, but let me give you the answer that seems reasonable in my mind.

The trustees are ultimately responsible for the governance of the University. They take this duty seriously. It is a pontifical university.

The Holy Father issued an encyclical. Members of this faculty, following their professional discipline, and their own conscience, publicly expressed their differences with or reservations from this formal public papal teaching.

It would seem to me that the trustees have a problem, here.

If you want data, it would seem to me that all reasonable trustees would say, how do we handle this? What do we do? . . .

Anyhow, the meeting was convened, and I know, because many members of the Board were in communication with one another, and among them decided we should meet to discuss this.

So it seems to me the three specific things I would cite as an answer to your question were the issuance of the encyclical and its contents, the conflicting opinion of the theologians concerned, and the mode, the method which they used to express publicly their reservations about it. . . .

MR. HUNT: My question was who questioned [the dissenters' conduct] to the trustees . . .

BISHOP SHANNON: I don't know who. I say I am assuming that any number of them had many questions about this, other bishops, other theologians, pastors.

MR. HUNT: Is it correct that at the Board meeting of September 5, the data available to the Board were limited to statements by various trustees as to what they had heard, what had come to their attention, and what they thought about the statement of the theologians? Is that essentially correct?

BISHOP SHANNON: I don't get the focus of the question.

There was extended discussion throughout the morning of that meeting of the action of the theologians, the response that had been received by individual members from unspecified sources. I don't recall that they were named.

I am not trying to be evasive, here, but we are influenced by these things, telephone calls, friends, reports in the paper.

In addition, Cardinal O'Boyle produced at the meeting a letter, dated August 14, 1968, that he had received from the Vatican Secretary of State. The letter advised that action should be taken against any dissenters from the Encyclical who refused to recant. Cardinal O'Boyle swore those present to secrecy about the letter, and no mention was made of it in the official minutes of the meeting. Thus Bishop Shannon testified to the Inquiry Panel that

"There was no bill of particulars in the sense that a specific person, either in an ecclesiastical position, or a person in another position, had leveled charges and demanded that action be taken, or any kind of memorandum like that."

The committee assigned to draft the Trustees' press release reported the following set of priorities near mid-afternoon on September 5.

To express *fealty* to the Holy Father.
To show respect for academic freedom as understood in University circles.
To relate Catholic University to the Catholic conscience.
To subscribe to the right of due process.
To sustain the Chancellor's concern for safeguarding Catholic doctrine.
To defer to the hierarchy's magisterium.
To authorize the Acting Rector to initiate a formal inquiry in accord with due academic process.
To relate matters of doctrine to the American hierarchy.
To insure that University authority would not interfere with the academic work of the dissenters, who in turn would agree to desist from criticism of *Humanae Vitae,* and not teach contrary to the magisterium. (Emphasis supplied.)

The priorities settled on in the foregoing drafting instructions formed the basis of the final form of the press release, made public without comment by the Chairman of the Board, Dr. Carroll E. Hochwalt, at approximately 9:00 p.m. on September 5, (see Appendix B).[1] Bishops Shannon, Wright and Zaleski, Chairman of the Commission on Doctrine of the National Conference of Catholic Bishops, together with Mr. Lawrence Hickey of Chicago, were then appointed to prepare the final draft of the press statement.

In their press release, after an expression of loyalty to the Pope, the Trustees made a showing of respect for academic freedom: "the Board reaffirms the commitment of the Catholic University to accepted norms of academic freedom in the work of teaching and to the due process protective of such freedom." The Trustees expressed their determination that the dissenters' conduct had raised "serious questions," and the Acting Rector was directed to convene an Inquiry (through due academic process) to determine whether the dissenters had violated their responsibilities to the University. The Trustees reserved any "canonical decisions involving teachers of sacred science" and any "final judgments concerning theological teachings" to the bishops of the Church.

The Trustees further directed that any of the dissenting professors who could not agree to abstain from any public commentary "involving the name of the University," and "inconsistent with the pronouncements of the teaching authority established in the Church, above all, that of the Holy Father" was to be suspended without any provision for a hearing. This *ad hoc* code of silence concerning hierarchical pronouncements laid down by the Trustees was to govern for the course of the Inquiry. One of the Trustees had brought a manual of procedures in faculty discipline cases promulgated by AAUP. The Trustees stated that their threat of suspension was "in accord with" the stated norms of AAUP concerning suspension, citing the page number of the AAUP Manual in which those norms were set forth. The norms cited permit suspension only if "immediate harm" is threatened by the subject professor's continued teaching. The Trustees' press release concluded by citing the Trustees' intention to protect the faculty from "harm to their academic freedom" and also to protect the Catholic community from "harm to the authentic teaching of the Church."

The Trustees' press release showed their concern with the professors' "manner and mode" (the "style and method of organizing and publicizing their dissent . . . raised serious questions"). But that was not the Trustees' only interest (indeed, their reference to questions of "style and method" was introduced by the word, "moreover"). The Trustees were also concerned with the substance of the professors' assertion—the right to dissent itself. The Trustees directly challenged this right, disowning the dissenters ("they do not speak for the University"), both by calling for an Inquiry into their "declarations" (as well as their "actions") and by threatening to suspend anyone who exercised, in whatever manner and by whatever mode, the asserted right to dissent.

Ironically, while the Trustees were formulating their statement calling for an end to the dissent pending an inquiry into its legitimacy, the press relations officer of Catholic University was asking two of the dissenters if they wanted to go to the hotel where the Trustees were meeting and brief the members of the press on the issues involved in the controversy. It was from the news media that the professors began to learn of the fate that awaited them during the next academic year. The Trustees did not inform the professors concerned about their mandate of an Inquiry and their threat of suspension. They simply issued a press release. The dissenting professors learned about the Inquiry and suspension in the newspapers. The Trustees then dispersed, leaving the problem in the hands of Acting Rector Whalen.

The professors at the University who had subscribed to the Statement of dissent, confronted with the problems of the imminent Inquiry and the choice between suspension from teaching and silence, immediately consulted with the national office of AAUP in Washington. The professors were advised that, in view of the Trustees' actions of September 5, they should retain legal counsel in addition to the academic counseling services which AAUP would provide. The Washington Chapter of the American Civil Liberties Union was interested in the case, but the professors obtained the services of the New York law firm of Cravath, Swaine & Moore (one of whose partners is a brother of one of the dissenting theologians). Professor Robert K. Webb, Professor of History at Columbia University, and Managing Editor of the *American Historical Review,* agreed to serve as the professors' academic counsel. The professors and their counsel were initially confronted with the question of whether to challenge or cooperate with the Inquiry. This question was intimately related to the choice of suspension or silence as proposed by the Trustees.

The University's academic year was about to begin. The Acting Rector, in order to determine who would be available to teach when classes opened in late September, began calling in each of the dissenting theologians to explain to them the Trustees' conditions of silence and to ask for their assent. Whalen presented each of the dissenting professors who were then on the campus with four written questions purporting to represent the mind of the Trustees on the matter, including, as the first question: "Do you intend to continue in your public opposition to the authentic teaching of the Magisterium as that opposition is set forth in your statement of July 30?" Rector Whalen also asked each professor, in this set of questions, whether he would agree to the conditions of silence proposed by the Trustees. The professors refused to respond in any manner to the question calling for a retraction of their dissent. To have answered that question, as framed, in either the affirmative *or* the negative, would have implied that the previous conduct of the professors had in fact been in opposition to the authentic teaching of the Church—a proposition with which they did not agree. Whalen soon revised this question to ask merely whether any of the subject professors wished to withdraw his subscription to the Theologians' Statement. None of the professors agreed to recant.

The conditions of silence were also unacceptable to the professors, who viewed them as nothing other than an *ad hoc* rule of conduct imposed by the Trustees without adequate consultation of the faculty and as lacking all basis in AAUP norms of academic freedom and academic due process which allow for no censorship of faculty expression. Bishop James Shannon explained during the Inquiry that the Trustees had asked the three faculty "representatives" present on September 5 whether they could "stand with" the Trustees' press release. He testified: "We asked the only members of this faculty we had who were accountable to their conferees back home, do you think this is reasonable, would this be acceptable, could you sell this to your faculty and still keep your self-respect, and they all said, yes, we think this is a very reasonable way to go about it. . . . Every member there gave personal testimony, that is in the record, not only accepting it, but commending it."

The "record" (the official minutes of the September 5 meeting) shows only that "representatives of the faculty . . . participated vigorously and were listened to respectfully." Nor were the faculty

members present authorized to speak for the dissenting professors
(Professor Curran had specifically told them so before the Trustees' meeting); nor were they in any way "accountable" to their
colleagues. How they came to be at the meeting is worthy of a
slight digression.

Faculty representatives to the Board of Trustees were an innovation at Catholic University resulting directly from the "Curran
affair" in 1967. Part of the settlement arrived at in the April 24,
1967, meeting of the faculty of the School of Theology with Chancellor O'Boyle was that a meeting of elected representatives of
the entire University faculty should be arranged with the Trustees
as soon as possible. On the morning of May 27, 1967, a Special
Committee of the Board of Trustees, presided over by Chancellor
O'Boyle, met with the faculty of Theology to discuss the relationship of theologians to the American Bishops. On the same afternoon elected representatives of the entire faculty met with the
Trustees' Committee to discuss the underlying problems at the
University, since they saw that the attempted dismissal of Professor Curran was merely a symptom of deeper communications
difficulties. At that session the Faculty Committee submitted and
explained four "demands": A new rector, reconstitution of the
Board of Trustees, reconstitution of the Academic Senate, and
direct faculty representation to the Board of Trustees on all
matters pertaining to the faculty. During the academic year 1967-
68, the Survey and Objectives Committee of the Board of Trustees,
chaired by Dr. Carroll A. Hochwalt of St. Louis, met regularly
with elected representatives of the faculty to implement the original
faculty demands. An arrangement was worked out whereby each
group of Schools of the University (Arts and Sciences, Professional and Ecclesiastical) would elect one representative who
thenceforth would sit with voice but no vote with the Board of
Trustees in all matters pertaining to the faculty. No specifics were
implemented concerning the precise role of these representatives;
no provision was made for "reporting" to the faculties they
represented. In fact, a private agreement was made between the
three elected faculty members and the Trustees that a prudent con-

fidentiality would be maintained. Since no provision was made either for instruction of the representatives by the faculties they represented or for reporting back to these faculties, these three professors were "representatives" only in an extremely limited sense. Obviously, during the course of the meeting, the three faculty members did not have an opportunity to consult with their colleagues or, in particular, with the dissenting professors, about the procedures under discussion; nor did the Trustees request them to do so or provide time for such consultation before the final vote on the press release was taken.

Acting Rector Whalen brought one or another of the faculty representatives with him (as he put it, to "keep him honest") at his meetings with the dissenters on September 9 and 10. He made clear to the dissenters that not only would any professor who agreed to be *silent* be spared the suspension, but also that any professor who agreed to *recant* would be spared the Inquiry and the suspension. This latter alternative emphasized to the professors the Trustees' challenge to the right to dissent itself, not merely the "manner and mode" of exercise of that right: if all the professors had retracted their dissent, there would have been no Inquiry into the "manner and mode" that the Trustees had termed seriously questionable.

The dissenting professors, mindful of the successful boycott at the University during the "Curran affair", were anxious to return to the classroom, where their position would be much stronger in any confrontation that might come. As a consequence, the professors and their counsel were forced to make some arrangements respecting the pending order of suspension. However, they could not agree to abstain from actions "inconsistent" with the teaching authority established in the Church, any more than they could respond to the question first posed by Acting Rector Whalen ("Do you intend to continue in your public opposition . . .?"). They did not believe they were inconsistent with Church teaching; indeed, they had asserted and offered scholarly support for the proposition that the right to dissent was "common teaching" in the Church.

The professors, through their counsel, therefore affirmed to the University administration that they could not accept the conditions proposed by the Trustees without qualification: the professors would agree only that the applicability of the Trustees' conditions would be governed by generally accepted norms of academic freedom, specifically, those of AAUP. They also agreed, pursuant to AAUP provisions governing the conduct of faculty disciplinary hearings, to abstain from any public comment concerning the proceedings of the Inquiry itself, pending its conclusion. An agreement was thereby concluded between the professors and the University administration, announced in a University Press Release of September 13, 1968, to the effect that the Trustees' mandate of silence would be effective only in so far as it was consistent with AAUP principles of responsible academic procedure, and that the professors would not be suspended. The University community from that time forward understood that the professors' obligation of "silence" related *only* to the ban on *Inquiry publicity* set down by AAUP, and not to the ban on acts of dissent put forth by the Trustees on September 5.[2]

Acting Rector Whalen asked the assistance of the University's Academic Senate in carrying out his mandate to initiate an Inquiry. The Academic Senate, a body composed of the deans of all the Schools of the University, of elected faculty representatives from each School and of certain administrative officers (*ex officio*), appointed two committees: "Committee A," under the chairmanship of Professor J. Kerby Neill, was directed to review and interpret the terms of the agreement respecting the Trustees suspension-or-silence conditions which was reached between Rector Whalen and the dissenting professors: "Committee B," under the chairmanship of Dean Donald E. Marlowe of the School of Engineering and Architecture, was charged with drawing up the procedures for the Inquiry.

Committee A's initial review of the agreement concerning the Trustees' conditions concluded that the agreement itself had been reached in accordance with due academic procedures; this initial review passed no judgment on the substance or the propriety of the condition of silence proposed by the Trustees.[3]

The professors' counsel were asked by Committee "B" to make proposals as to the conduct of the Inquiry. In response, they submitted a draft set of procedures based primarily on the guidelines recommended by AAUP in its 1958 Statement of Procedural Standards in Faculty Dismissal Proceedings.

The 1958 Statement postulates that no proceedings questioning or examining the conduct of faculty members should be instituted unless there is reason to question such faculty member's fitness to teach under accepted norms of responsible academic procedure. Beginning at this point, the 1958 Statement set forth a simple, three-stage procedure for cases involving questions concerning faculty conduct:

1) When reason arises to question the fitness of a faculty member to teach, the president or administrative head of the university conducts a personal study of the matter. This confidential study is "stage one" of the proceedings.

2) Where the administration cannot effect a settlement of the matter through its good offices, an inquiry committee elected from among the faculty of the university is to be impaneled to effect such a settlement or to determine whether formal proceedings to consider dismissal should be instituted. This confidential faculty inquiry is "stage two."

3) If either the inquiry committee or the administrative head of the university determines that formal dismissal proceedings should be instituted, charges are formulated and written notice of such charges is sent to the subject professor, initiating "stage three," that is, formal dismissal hearings. The report of the dismissal hearing committee, to be elected by the university faculty, is to be forwarded to the trustees either to accept or remand. It is generally only in the third stage of the actual formal hearing that the possibility of suspension of a faculty member comes into play—such suspension must, as noted in connection with the Trustees' press release, be based on a threat of immediate danger caused by the teacher's continuing presence in the classroom.

Although the Catholic University Trustees called for a mere Inquiry (which would normally correspond to the confidential, "grand-jury" style proceedings at "stage two" of AAUP's disciplinary procedures), the Trustees had nonetheless called on the Inquiry body to report back to *them,* and to determine whether or not the professors had "violated their responsibilities," not simply whether there was reasonable cause to believe that the professors had violated their responsibilities and had thus given cause for formal dismissal hearings. Moreover, the Trustees had specifically invoked the suspension arrangement sanctioned by AAUP for use when serious formal charges were to be made. Counsel for the professors thus recommended that the relatively formal hearing procedures of "stage three" be adopted in the Inquiry.

Counsel for the professors were also concerned about three possible unfavorable outcomes of the Inquiry process—one was that the Trustees would dismiss out of hand whatever conclusions were reached by the Inquiry Committee as a "faculty white-wash"; another was that the Trustees would find the faculty panel incompetent to pass on the theological questions necessarily related to the issues raised by the Trustees; another was that the Trustees would conclude that the Inquiry Board had not dealt with the particular conduct which was on the Trustees' minds on September 5 when they publicly called into question matters labeled only generally as "declarations or actions in respect of the Encyclical *Humanae Vitae*" and "organizing and publicizing" dissent. To counteract these possibilities, counsel focused on three basic objectives:

1) To assure that the structure and composition of the Inquiry Committee would reflect both the expertise essential to determining the difficult issues obviously within the scope of the Inquiry and the broad-based faculty participation called for under AAUP norms;

2) To assure that the Inquiry proceedings themselves, while not encumbered with technical rules of evidence or other customary courtroom procedures, would nonetheless be conducted with sufficient formality and regularity to prevent any subsequent im-

peachment of the record of the Inquiry on the basis of prejudicial procedural defects; and

3) To make a representative of the Trustees a significant party to the Inquiry proceedings, so that charges might be proffered, witnesses might be presented, exhibits might be tendered, testimony might be submitted and findings might be proposed in a manner assuring full development of any issues which the Trustees wanted to be considered and assuring that the professors would not have the burden of proof.

As to the first matter: the recommendation of the professors' counsel was substantially accepted by Committee B and the Academic Senate. The Procedures for the Inquiry approved by the Academic Senate on October 16, 1968, called for a five-member Board of Inquiry. One member of the Board was to be elected by the Academic Senate from each of the three main divisions of the University (the Graduate Schools of Arts and Sciences, the Professional Schools and the Ecclesiastical Schools); two members were to be elected by the entire Senate "at large" (one of whom was to be from outside the University and competent in the sacred sciences); in addition, one alternate member of the Board was to be elected by the Senate from the University faculty "at large." Furthermore, the Inquiry Board was authorized to retain a technical staff, possibly to include independent experts, to render professional advice to the Board.

As to the second matter: the October 16 Rules of the Academic Senate provided the essential structures and elements of a fair hearing, including the right of each party to be represented by counsel; to be informed of the detailed procedural rules to be followed by the Inquiry Board; to attend all proceedings of the Inquiry Board other than its own deliberations; to call witnesses (including specially qualified "expert" witnesses); to have the assistance of the Inquiry Board to secure the attendance or written testimony of witnesses and to obtain production of pertinent documentary evidence; to question all witnesses testifying before the Inquiry Board; to propose findings to the Inquiry Board; to receive current copies of the transcript which was to be taken of all Inquiry Board hearings; and to have written notification of the findings of the Inquiry. The Senate provided that the University would pay the expenses of "expert" witnesses called by any party and not deemed merely cumulative by the Inquiry Board. The October 16 Rules also provided that the Inquiry Board would establish detailed rules of procedure and would hold pre-Inquiry conferences with the parties for the exchange of names of witnesses, documentary evidence and written testimony.

As to the third matter: counsel for the professors envisioned a "devil's advocate" party who would present to the Inquiry Board the charges portended by the Trustees' press statement of September 5 and who would focus the Inquiry Board's attention on the specific conduct to which those charges related. Committee B, however, was sensitive to the suggestion that the coming Inquiry would determine formal charges of misconduct. The Academic Senate's October 16 Rules made no mention of charges but, in Paragraph 5 (A) provided a "two-sided" structure to the Inquiry: the "parties" to the Inquiry were to consist of the dissenting professors *and,* as a *distinct* party, a person designated by the University administration who would "assure full and complete development of the issues" before the Inquiry Board.

Shortly after the adoption of the October 16 Rules, the Inquiry Board was elected. Its members were Dean Donald E. Marlowe of the School of Engineering and Architecture, Professor E. Catherine Dunn of the Department of English, Dean Frederick R. McManus of the School of Canon Law, Professor Antanas Suziedelis of the Department of Psychology and the Reverend Doctor Eugene I. Van Antwerp, Associate Secretary of the Seminary Department of the National Catholic Education Association. The alternate Board member was Professor Kenneth L. Schmitz of the Catholic University School of Philosophy. The Board elected Dean Marlowe as its Chairman and selected Mr. Alfred L. Scanlan of the Washington, D.C., law firm of Shea & Gardner as its counsel.[4]

Notes

1. Board of Trustees of The Catholic University of America Statement Concerning Dissenting Theologians at Catholic University, September 5, 1968.
2. See the 1940 Statement on Academic Freedom and Tenure (AAUP), more fully treated in chapter 4.
3. Report of "Committee A" of the Academic Senate of The Catholic University of America (March 6, 1969); this Report is more fully treated in chapter 5. The September 13 press release had stated that after "extended discussion . . . agreement was reached by all parties [specifying] that such conditions are to be interpreted and applied in accordance with the commitment of the University to accepted norms of Academic Freedom and due process, and the norms of the AAUP."
4. The Board of Inquiry also utilised the services of Professor James A. Coriden, from the School of Theology, who prepared background material on certain canonical matters.

3

The Trustees'
New Focus

"Hence the focus of the present inquiry is on the style and method whereby some faculty members expressed personal dissent from Papal teaching, and apparently helped organize additional public dissent to such teaching. At no time in this inquiry is there any attempt by the Board to question the right of a scholar to have or to hold private dissent on Papal teaching not defined as infallible."—Letter dated December 23, 1968, from Brother Nivard Scheel, C.F.X., Acting Rector of Catholic University, on behalf of the Board of Trustees, to the Chairman of the Faculty Board of Inquiry.

Notwithstanding the Trustees' public implicit condemnation of the position set forth in the Statement by Catholic Theologians, the right to dissent upheld by that Statement was having an important impact on the Church in many foreign countries and was not without impact on the Church in the United States. As of September 5, the American bishops had not publicly acknowledged the existing right of Catholics to dissent from noninfallible papal teachings such as *Humanae Vitae*. (The implicit recognition of this right in the bishops' original collective statement of July 31 released by Archbishop Dearden had been publicly repudiated almost immediately.) Individual bishop's statements spoke only of an obligation of *assent* to the papal teaching, consistent with the unnuanced presentation in the 1967 Pastoral Letter (with the notable exception of Bishop Charles Buswell of Pueblo, Colorado, who published an article in the November 15, 1968, issue of *Commonweal* which acknowledged a right of dissent from the Encyclical and criticized those who questioned the loyalty of dissenters).

Bishops in other countries and other national bishops' conferences, however, were beginning to articulate the right to dissent and its possible applicability in the case of *Humanae Vitae.* For example, on July 30, 1968, Cardinal Alfrink of the Netherlands publicly announced that Catholics do not have to accept the Encyclical without discussion or debate, and called an emergency conference of the Dutch hierarchy. On August 2, Cardinal Alfrink and six other Roman Catholic bishops of the Netherlands issued a joint letter with copies to the press to the effect that the Encyclical is not infallible, and that while "the personal conscience cannot pass over an authoritative pronouncement such as a papal letter . . . there are many factors which determine one's personal conscience regarding marriage rules (for example the mutual love, the relations in a family and the social circumstances)."[1] On August 30, at their conference at Malines, the Belgian hierarchy issued a statement to the Belgian Church and the press which included the following:

Someone, however, who is competent in the matter under consideration and capable of forming a personal and well-founded judgment—which necessarily presupposes a sufficient amount of knowledge —may, after a serious examination before God, come to other conclusions on certain points. In such a case he has the right to follow his conviction provided that he remains sincerely disposed to continue his enquiry.[2] A similar doctrine, which we find also in St. Thomas Aquinas (*Ia, IIae,* q. 13, a.5) inspires the conciliar Declaration on Religious Freedom (*Dign. Hum.,* nos. 2 & 3).

Also on August 30, at Koenigstein, Federal Republic of Germany, the German hierachy issued to the German Church and to the press a statement concerning the Encyclical which included the following:

On the other hand, we know that many are of the opinion that they cannot accept the encyclical's statement on the methods of regulating births. They are convinced that this is the exceptional case of which we have spoken in our doctrinal letter of last year. As far as we can see the main questions voiced are: Is the teaching tradition obligatory on the decision stated in the encyclical; do not the recently prominently stressed aspects of marriage and its consummation, also mentioned in the encyclical, cast a doubt on the decisions rendered on the methods of birth control.

He who believes that he must think this way must examine himself conscientiously to determine whether or not he is free of subjective pride and arrogance so that he can account for his position before the judgment of God. In adopting this position he will have to give consideration to the laws of intra-Church dialogue and try to avoid giving any scandal. Only the person acting in such a manner can avoid conflict with the properly understood obligation due authority and the duty of obedience. Only in that way does he contribute to their Christian understanding and realization.[3]

However, two days after the Catholic University Trustees' meeting of September 5, it was reported that Archbishop Luigi Raimondi, the "Apostolic Delegate" of the Vatican residing in Washington, D.C., had written a general letter to the American hierarchy asserting that it was of the "utmost importance" that the dissent from *Humanae Vitae* be quieted down immediately.[4] In the United States at least, hierarchical recognition of the legitimacy of dissent was to be a long and difficult process (indeed, a process not yet completed).

On September 17, one week after the Acting Rector of Catholic University, on behalf of its Trustees, was asking the dissenting professors at that University to recant and be silent, Bishop Zaleski (a Trustee of the University who served as a final draftsman of the Trustees' September 5 press release), as Chairman of the National Conference of Catholic Bishops' Commission on Doctrine, delivered a confidential report on the question of dissent to the Executive Committee of the Bishops' Conference. His report informed the bishops that "It is possible that a person in good faith may be unable to give internal assent to an encyclical"[5] and that this right of dissent applied to "any Catholic"[6] thus not simply to theologians but to married Catholics practically concerned with the question of artificial contraception. Bishop Zaleski proposed guidelines for the "voicing" of dissent from an encyclical, observing that "A person in good faith . . . must beware of voicing dissent in the wrong way":

> Dissent can be expressed but it must be done in a manner becoming to a docile believer and a loyal son of the church.
> Such dissent must show that it is an expression from a believing person—a man of faith.
> Such dissent can only be expressed in a manner which does not disturb the conscience of other believing people.
> Dissent must be accompanied by an open mind and a willingness to alter one's view in the light of new evidence.
> *Such dissent must be brought to the proper authorities in the proper manner and quietly.*[7] (Emphasis supplied.)

On that same day the Acting Rector of Catholic University sent a "Special Communication to the Bishops of the United States" to bring them "up to date on the events of the last month and a half" at the University. He informed the bishops of his efforts in arranging the August 19 meeting at the Statler-Hilton among some of the dissenters and bishops and theologians who disagreed with the dissent. He then revealed that

> . . . I received calls from the presidents of other Catholic colleges and universities who wanted to talk about the problem as it affected their own faculty members who signed the statement. I told them there would be a Trustee meeting at Catholic University and they felt they would like to wait and see the outcome of this meeting before taking any steps, if they would take any at all. Cardinal O'Boyle and Dr. Hochwalt sent you the resolution of the Trustees after the meeting of September 5. I received a directive from them to be certain that there would be no action on the part of the C.U. faculty that would be in opposition to the authentic teaching of the Church (which I feel a conscientious obligation to do anyway). If the faculty members could not agree to this in the present case, I was directed to suspend them from teaching during the course of an inquiry, which I was directed to undertake immediately. I had interviews with these men individually and they agreed to the conditions outlined by the Trustees.

The Acting Rector made no mention in his communication to the bishops of the University press release of September 13 which had noted the qualifications to the applicability of the condition of silence "outlined by the Trustees" with the mandatory reference to AAUP norms.

Neither Bishop Zaleski's expression on the right of "any Catholic . . . in good faith" to dissent, nor Acting Rector Whalen's letter was then made public or known to the professors and their counsel. The first public knowledge of the fact that the American bishops were privately informed by Bishop Zaleski on September 17 of the applicability of the right to dissent to persons in good faith came after the conclusion of the Inquiry at Catholic University (in the late spring of 1969). The first knowledge the subject professors had of a possible shift in the position of the United States hierarchy concerning the legitimacy of dissent was the publication of the Pastoral Letter *Human Life In Our Day* on November 15, 1968. In light of present knowledge of Bishop Zaleski's report to the Bishops' Commission on Doctrine on September 17 (acknowledging a right of dissent on the part of "any Catholic"), the Pastoral Letter appears to have been something of a victory for conservative bishops insofar as its only explicit acknowledgment of the right to dissent is phrased as applicable to professional theological scholars. However, the exact phrasing of the Pastoral Letter is not without ambiguity:

There exists in the Church a lawful freedom of inquiry and of thought and also general norms of licit dissent. This is particularly true in the area of legitimate theological speculation and research. When conclusions reached by such professional theological work prompt a scholar to dissent from noninfallible received teaching the norms of that dissent come into play.

Relevant to the issue of the manner and mode of the subject professors' dissent is the assertion of the Pastoral Letter that the norms of licit dissent "will not necessarily require the responsible scholar to relinquish his opinion but certainly to propose it with prudence. . . ." Bear in mind that the Theologians' Statement did not merely express speculative dissent from the Encyclical; rather, it affirmed that "spouses may responsibly decide according to their conscience" to dissent from the Encyclical in practice.

On November 19, John Cardinal Krol, Archbishop of Philadelphia and a Trustee of Catholic University, issued a pastoral letter in connection with an appeal for funds for Catholic University. He spoke of the dissent as an "unprecedented rejection of the teaching of the Vicar of Christ" which was "widely publicized to the shock and indignation of many":

The resentment of some was directed not toward the dissenters but toward the University. The dissenters number 21—the faculty numbers 624. The Board of Trustees declared that the dissenters do not speak for the University and affirmed full adherence to the teaching authority of the Pope. The Board did not permit the dissenters to teach unless they agreed to abstain from anything inconsistent with the pronouncements of the teaching authority in the Church. The Rector was instructed to suspend any teacher who would not agree to or would not so abstain.

Cardinal Krol stated that "It is most regrettable that . . . the loyalty of the faithful to the University has been put to such a cruel test." He urged the Catholics in his archdiocese to continue to contribute to the University in light of his "conviction that Catholic doctrine will be vindicated." Publication of the Krol letter indicated that the Cardinal was unaware of the emasculation of the Trustees' conditions for continued teaching at the University and, upon investigation, the subject professors obtained (in early December), a copy of the Whalen letter of September 17.

Thus, by the time of the first pre-inquiry conference on December 13, so far as the subject professors were aware:

(1) The national hierarchies of several foreign countries had publicly issued statements consistent with the Theologians' Statement (although, notwithstanding this evidence of the Catholic legitimacy of the right to dissent established by those hierarchies, the Chancellor of Catholic University, Cardinal O'Boyle, in his capacity as Archbishop of Washington, had suspended the priestly

faculties, in whole or in part, of a large number of priests under his ecclesiastical jurisdiction who had done nothing more than acknowledge that they would respect this Catholic option in their pastoral work).

2) The American hierarchy, in their 1968 Pastoral Letter, had affirmed the right of a scholar to engage in "speculative" dissent, at times even publicly.

3) The American hierarchy had been informed by the Administration of Catholic University that the dissenting professors of the University had agreed to abstain from any pronouncements inconsistent with the teachings of the hierarchy and the Pope, as those conditions of silence were outlined by the Trustees of Catholic University on September 5, whereas the professors had not so agreed.

In the context of these developments, the professors and their counsel came to feel that it was more imperative than ever that the "devil's advocate" party, provided by the October 16 Rules of the Academic Senate, be quickly designated so that he could provide "complete and thorough amplification of the issues before the Board of Inquiry."

The new Acting Rector of the University, Brother Nivard Scheel, C.F.X., who had assumed office the day before the Academic Senate's October 16 Rules were approved, assured the professors' counsel in late November that the party contemplated by Rule 5 (A) would be designated. During the first week of December, however, counsel for the professors learned that the "other party" to the Inquiry had not yet been designated; at about the same time, they received a copy of the "December 6 Rules" of the Board of Inquiry, which reflected the absence of the other party by calling on the *professors* to initiate the hearing process by submitting "a written response to the questions raised by the Board of Trustees," without any further articulation of the Trustees' concerns of September 5 or any charges or other presentation by the party who was to represent the Trustees according to Senate Rule 5 (A). This attempt to put the burden on the "subject professors" to set forth a statement of relevant facts and positions regarding the September 5 "questions" indicated that, without formal charges or a party who would particularize the Trustees' concerns, the professors would necessarily bear the burden of proving their innocence. This was particularly true because the Inquiry which the Trustees mandated was not to be simply a "fact-finding" process, but was specifically directed to determine whether the professors had "violated their responsibilities"—a "guilty" or "innocent" judgment.

When the Inquiry Board Chairman convened the first pre-Inquiry conference at 3:00 p.m. on December 13, 1968, there was no "other" party present as contemplated by Rule 5 (A) of the Academic Senate. None had been appointed or designated. The Chairman's agenda had contemplated that "the parties" would begin preliminary discussions concerning the issues before the Inquiry Board, but counsel for the professors pointed out that any such discussions would be fruitless without the presence of the other party, and observed that the structure of the December 6 Rules unfairly left the "subject professors" with the burden of proving their innocence.

Legal counsel for the University Trustees were in attendance at the December 13 conference, and objected to any suggestion that the Inquiry should become an adversary hearing. Counsel for the professors agreed that it was not contemplated that the University or the University Administration, as such, would be an adversary party in the Inquiry proceedings, but affirmed that someone should come forward to explain what the Trustees were concerned with on September 5 and that such function was the task of the party to be appointed under Senate Rule 5 (A). Counsel for the University Trustees agreed that such a party could be designated by the Acting Rector, but no one explained why there had been no designation.

The attorney who had been retained by the Inquiry Board as a member of its technical staff stated that someone would have to furnish the other side or the "other party" to serve the role of a "devil's advocate." The professors' counsel affirmed that the professors would not participate unless the other party was designated and unless further specification of the issues on the minds of the Trustees was provided.

Surprised by the turn of events, the Inquiry Board recessed briefly and emerged from a private conference to announce its decision "to request the [Acting] Rector to designate a person or persons as referred to in [Rule 5 (A) of the Academic Senate] who will be authorized to clarify or particularize the issues raised by the Board of Trustees in its September 5, 1968, statement." The Acting Rector, who was present, indicated that he would comply with the Inquiry Board's request, and the professors' counsel indicated that they would be satisfied so long as the party designated would specify which Statutes, By-laws or rules of the University, and which norms of responsible academic procedure, formed the basis for the questions raised by the Trustees on September 5.

The Board of Trustees, however, through its Chairman and a special committee including Bishop Shannon, Cardinal Krol and Archbishop Hannan, together with a non-Trustee, Bishop Wright, decided to respond to the Inquiry Board's request for clarification or particularization of the September 5 press release through a letter of comment on behalf of the Trustees released to the Inquiry Board over signature of the Acting Rector on December 23, 1968, (see Appendix C). The Inquiry Board Chairman informed the professors' counsel of this development. Counsel replied that the professors would not proceed without the other party contemplated by Senate Rule 5 (A). The Acting Rector subsequently announced the designation of Bishop Shannon as the party contemplated by Senate Rule 5 (A).

The December 23 letter of comment from the Trustees denied that their September 5 statement made or portended any charges or accusations and affirmed that their threat of suspension was meant as a charitable call for truce. The Trustees confessed that they were unaware of *the existence* of norms of "responsible faculty procedure endorsed by American universities in matters of public debate or controversy," even though, on September 5, they had asserted unequivocally that the dissent of the subject profes-

sors had "raised serious questions" in terms of "responsible academic procedure."

The Trustees asserted that they had never challenged the
scholar's right to dissent in the first place: "At no time in this
inquiry is there any attempt by the Board [of Trustees] to question the right of a scholar to have or to hold private dissent on
Papal teaching not defined as infallible." The Trustees made no
mention of and gave no explanation of the fact that Acting Rector
Whalen, on behalf of the Trustees, had informed the dissenting
professors that anyone who recanted his dissent would be spared
the Inquiry.

The December 23 letter purported to set forth the sources of the
objections and concerns which motivated the Trustees to call for
the Inquiry into the dissent.

First of all, the concern of the Board of Trustees in the current
world-wide discussion of our Holy Father's Encyclical, *Humanae
Vitae*, arises from the fact that this Board is ultimately responsible for
the policies which guide The Catholic University of America and also
responsible to Our Holy Father, Pope Paul VI, as the Supreme Teacher
in the Catholic Church. The public action of certain faculty members
from The Catholic University challenging the doctrine of a Papal
Encyclical has *caused many persons in the Church and many others*
to question the propriety, according to accepted academic standards,
of the action of these professors. There are several publics to which
the governing board of any university must account. In the current
instance, *many of these constituencies (including the general faculty
of the University itself) have been puzzled by the manner in which
some professors* on the faculty of The Catholic University of America
*have publicly promulgated their dissent from a Papal Encyclical and
have apparently undertaken to organize public opposition* to this teaching. *Some have expressed puzzlement not only because of the suddenness with which these actions were undertaken, but also because they
seemed to some to be done without a proper regard for the person of
the Holy Father and for the pastoral implications involved.* [Emphasis
supplied.]

Counsel for the professors asked Bishop Shannon to explain

this passage when he appeared to testify at the pre-Inquiry conference of January 10, 1969. Bishop Shannon testified that he could not name (because he did not know) those "many persons in the Church and many others" who had questioned the propriety of the professors' dissent according to accepted academic standards; nor could he name any members of the "general faculty of the University itself" who were "puzzled" by the manner in which the professors publicly promulgated their dissent and apparently undertook "to organize public opposition" to the Encyclical, or who "expressed puzzlement" because of the suddenness of the dissent; nor could he name those who were puzzled because the dissent "seemed to be done without a proper regard for the person of the Holy Father." Neither Bishop Shannon nor the December 23 letter particularized further the specific nature of the general "questions" and "puzzlement." As noted in Chapter Two, Bishop Shannon testified that there was no expression of specifics of such concerns at the Trustees' meeting of September 5, but that the members of the Board acted under the influence of unspecified telephone calls, friends and reports in the newspapers.

The Trustees' December 23 letter and Bishop Shannon's testimony made clear that the Trustees were not going to make charges or otherwise particularize their "questions" of September 5. The professors subject to the Inquiry, therefore, had to choose between the risks of declining active participation in the Inquiry and the burdens of assuming the task of proving their "responsibility." They chose the latter course and their task absorbed an entire academic year (including the time spent between September and the beginning of the Inquiry hearings in January). The professors and their counsel spent over 10,000 hours preparing and conducting their case, and spent over $8,000 in payment for the costs of transportation, telephone consultation and production and reproduction of materials incident to the Inquiry.

Since the Trustees did not specify the dissenting conduct of the professors that was the object of their concern, other than in general terms, the professors were constrained to prepare a full chronology of the conduct of each of them in respect to *Humanae Vitae* between the dates of July 29 (the issuance of the Encyclical) and September 5 (the issuance of the Trustees' press release calling for the Inquiry). Furthermore, in order to put these facts in their proper context, the professors dealt with related matters going back two years or more. The professors submitted this chronology of their actions as a 96-page proposed Stipulation of Facts (supplemented by a 40-page annex of Exhibits) to the Inquiry Board in late January. After the Inquiry Board and Bishop Shannon (on behalf of the Trustees) had had an opportunity to question the professors concerning the proposed Stipulation, it was adopted, with minor clarifying changes, as Findings of Fact by the Inquiry Board, with the agreement of the subject professors and Bishop Shannon, as of February 5, 1969.[8]

As the Inquiry Board then proceeded to hold hearings to prepare for its judgment on the facts as found, the professors submitted the first part of their written testimony—over 250 pages of materials, prepared in collaboration among the twenty professors and with assistance of counsel. Those materials, set forth in the companion volume to this work, were addressed to the issue of the professional competence of the subject professors as Roman Catholic theologians and defended on Roman Catholic theological principles their action in publicly upholding the right to dissent from *Humanae Vitae*. After the Inquiry Board had an opportunity to read these materials and question the professors about them, counsel for the professors submitted, on behalf of the professors, the second part of their prepared testimony—over 150 pages of materials defending the responsibility of the professors' conduct in light of the existing norms of responsible academic procedure and in light of their existing duties under the Statutes and other regulations of the University. The latter materials, set forth in the following five chapters, provided the background for the expert testimony of academicians attesting to the professors' innocence of any professional wrongdoing. Excerpts from this expert testimony are also included in the following chapters. At the conclusion of the Inquiry, the professors each volunteered their individual testimony as to the reasons for their dissent and as to the burdens which the Inquiry proceedings placed upon them during the preceding months; they also submitted themselves to unrestricted questioning by the members of the Inquiry Board, representatives of the administration and counsel for the Trustees. In this context, the professors and their counsel asked the Board of Inquiry to examine not only the responsibility of the professors' conduct, but also the propriety of the University Trustees' actions in mandating the Inquiry and threatening to suspend any professor who did not cease his public dissent from the Encyclical.

Notes

1. *New York Times,* August 3, 1968, p. 1.
2. National Catholic News Service (Foreign), September 4, 1968.
3. National Catholic News Service (Foreign), September 11, 1968.
4. *The Baltimore Sun,* September 7, 1968, § B, p. 20.
5. Letter dated September 23, 1968, from Most Rev. James P. Shannon to His Holiness, Pope Paul VI, citing the report of Bishop Zaleski, as reprinted in The *National Catholic Reporter,* June 4, 1969, p. 9, cols. 2–4.
6. *Ibid.*
7. *Ibid.*
8. Exhibit 8, Record of The Faculty Board of Inquiry, on file in the Archives of The Catholic University of America.

4

The Inquiry:
The Rationale
of Academic Freedom

"Timidity must not lead the scholar to stand silent when he ought to speak, particularly in the field of his competence. In matters of conscience and when he has the truth to proclaim the scholar has no obligation to be silent in the face of popular disapproval."—American Association of Universities' Statement on Academic Freedom and Responsibility, 1953.

The modern American university, like the Catholic Church, has been in the vortex of the challenging protests and dissents against the established institutional patterns of the present age. Indeed, the assertions of many of these contemporary protests are precisely that extant institutions such as the Church and the university have strayed from their core purposes and have catered to particular interests irrelevant to those purposes, but some of the dissenters and protesters themselves have been accused of violating the very same fundamental principles which they seek to uphold. In this context, it is necessary to study the dissent at Catholic University in the light of relevant fundamental concepts and values.

The university is the principal institution in Western society whose purpose is to search for and transmit truth regardless of all competing and conflicting pressures and demands; as such, it is the chief instrument whereby society provides itself with a continuous flow of ideas and with independent criticism and advice.

If the university is to be effective in providing intellectual and technological foundations for a complex modern society, and if it is to continue to perform its further role as an independent source of criticism and conscience in society, it must be free to fix its own standards and determine its own criteria for selecting its members.[1] The university is, as the Trustees of Catholic University, for example, have recognized and declared, "essentially a free and autonomous center of study and an agency serving the needs of human society."[2] Within the proper atmosphere of an academic community, "the only constraint upon truth is truth itself."[3]

It is within the context of the recognized purpose of a university "to search out truth scientifically, to safeguard it, and to apply it to the molding and shaping of both private and public life"[4] that the concept of academic freedom has been asserted and recognized. As a means to truth, academic freedom is neither an end nor an absolute; it is neither secular nor profane. It is recognized from a variety of perspectives: an article in *The New Catholic Encyclopedia* considers academic freedom to be simply man's God-given intellectual freedom specified in the university context;[5] similarly, the *Harvard Law Review* has recently described academic freedom as "that aspect of intellectual liberty concerned with the peculiar institutional needs of the academic community."[6] In the Introduction to its exhaustive review of developments in the law with respect to academic freedom, the *Review* concisely summarizes the essential aspects of the concept of academic freedom:

> The claim that scholars are entitled to particular immunity from ideological coercion is premised on a conception of the university as a community of scholars engaged in the pursuit of knowledge, collectively and individually, both within the classroom and without, and on the pragmatic conviction that the invaluable service rendered by the university to society can be performed only in an atmosphere entirely free from administrative, political, or ecclesiastical constraints on thought and expression.[7]

A distinguished former President of the American Association of University Professors, Professor Ralph Fuchs, confirms the accepted understanding of academic freedom, its basic philosophy and function:

> Academic freedom is that freedom of members of the academic community, assembled in colleges and universities, which underlies the effective performance of their functions of teaching, learning, practice of the arts, and research. The right to academic freedom is recognized in order to enable faculty members and students to carry on their roles. It is not sought as a personal privilege . . . .[8]

Professor Fuchs has pointed out that the concept of academic freedom recognized in colleges and universities in the United States today rests basically on three foundations:

1) the idea of intellectual freedom, which originated in Greece, rose again in medieval Europe, was reinforced during the Renaissance and came to maturity in the eighteenth century;

2) the idea of autonomy for communities of scholars, which arose in the universities of Europe; and

3) the freedoms guaranteed by the Bill of Rights of the Federal Constitution as elaborated by the courts.[9]

The *Harvard Law Review* study indicates how the American experience has contrasted the European societies whose "academic freedom of the university professor protected him only in the classroom, and not against repressive conditions outside the university walls," with the American experience "wherein academic freedom has grown to incorporate the right of the professor to speak openly in his private capacity without fear of adverse consequence within his university."[10] Professors Richard Hofstadter and Walter P. Metzger, the authors of a major treatise on the development of academic freedom in the United States, further specifically differentiate the American development in respect of extramural freedom from the German concept, which had been characterized by a close interrelationship of teaching freedom and learning freedom. They note the similarity of American and German norms for intramural activities, but conclude that "outside the University, for professors in their civil roles, the American norm was more permissive than the German, because it reflected a stronger social and constitutional commitment to free speech."[11]

The development of principles of freedom of speech, expression and association in the American legal forum has contributed a substantial content to the working principles of academic freedom (although academic freedom itself does not depend conceptually on constitutional protections). Our highest courts have recognized and given effect to the concept of academic freedom. In *Sweezy v. New Hampshire,* a majority of the Supreme Court of the United States asserted:

> The essentiality of freedom in the community of American universities is almost self-evident. . . . Scholarship cannot flourish in an atmosphere of suspicion and distrust. Teachers and students must always remain free to inquire, to study and to evaluate, to gain new maturity and understanding; otherwise our civilization will stagnate and die.[12]

The Court recently reaffirmed the importance of academic freedom in *Keyishian v. Board of Education*:

> Our Nation is deeply committed to safeguarding academic freedom, which is of transcendent value to all of us and not merely to the teachers concerned. That freedom is therefore a special concern of the First Amendment, which does not tolerate laws that cast a pall of orthodoxy over the classroom. . . . The Nation's future depends upon leaders trained through wide exposure to that robust exchange of ideas which discovers truth "out of a multitude of tongues, [rather] than through any kind of authoritative selection."[13]

In his concurring opinion in *Sweezy v. New Hampshire,* Justice Felix Frankfurter expressed the matter most succinctly:

> It is the business of a university to provide that atmosphere which is most conducive to speculation, experiment and creation. It is an atmosphere in which there prevail "the four essential freedoms" of a university—to determine for itself on academic grounds, who may teach, what may be taught, how it shall be taught, and who may be admitted to study.[14]

The legal protections that have developed, however, do not provide the totality of safeguards needed by the university professor in his pursuit of truth. Academic freedom requires special protections additional to those provided by the freedom of speech guaranteed by the Constitution:

> . : . Professors need more than this absence of governmental sanctions, more than a guarantee that they will not be jailed for the expressions of their thoughts. . . . The dismissal of a professor from his post not only prevents him from performing his function in society, but, by intimidating thousands of others and causing them to be satisfied with "safe" subjects and "safe" opinions, it also prevents the entire profession from effectively performing its function.
>
> . . . The occupational work of the vast majority of people is largely independent of their thought and speech. The professor's work *consists* of his thought and speech. If he loses his position for what he writes or says, he will, as a rule, have to leave his profession, and may no longer be able effectively to question and challenge accepted doctrines or effectively to defend challenged doctrines. And if *some* professors lose their positions for what they write or say, the effect on many other professors will be such that their usefulness to their students and to society will be gravely reduced.[15]

Some contend, however, that the notion that the institutional position of professors should not be affected by what they utter publicly provides teachers with immunity from economic penalties other citizens suffer as a result of unpopular expressions: loss of employment, loss of clients, boycotts of products and the like. But American academic institutions have recognized that their own neutrality, which is essential to their role in society, would be jeopardized if they attempt to constrain the expressions of faculty members: "If a university or college censors what its professors may say . . . it thereby assumes responsibility for what it permits them to say . . . a responsibility which an institution of learning would be very unwise in assuming."[16] Thus, academic freedom is asserted and defended not simply in the interest of professors, but in the interest of the university community and of American society.[17] Academic freedom is an essential element of society that is committed to the norm of freedom.[18] As the members of the Association of American Universities (AAU) have insisted:

> . . . Freedom of thought and speech is vital to the maintenance of the American system and is essential to the general welfare. . . . To insist upon conformity to current beliefs and practices will do infinite harm to the principle of freedom, which is the greatest, the central, American doctrine. Fidelity to that principle has made it possible for the universities of America to confer great benefits upon our society and our country. Adherence to that principle is the only guarantee that this nation may continue to enjoy those benefits.[19]

The present American commitment to defend academic freedom did not, of course, "spring full-blown from the soil in which our education grew in this country"[20]

> It evolved, rather, along with specific protections to academic freedom, from the organizational forms and educational policies that arose in colleges and universities, and from struggles over recurring infringements of freedom or tenure, which sometimes took the form of faculty dismissals.[21]

Many of these infringements were the work of administrative officers or boards, moved in most instances by the climate of opinion outside the university. The notion that infringements of academic freedom always involve governments or trustees as the oppressors, however, would be a stereotype:

> Far from seeing boards of trustees as the main sources of infringements of academic freedom in the United States, one may regard them ideally as the chief protectors of academic freedom against pressures from the outside, from political or ecclesiastical quarters, from civic organizations, or from private interest groups. . . .
> . . . [T]rustees and administrators, no less than sovereigns and governors, should share with professors and students in the defense of academic freedom. And such defense may be needed against pressures from all quarters—including professors themselves. In short, academic freedom implies protection from pressures and from attempts to intimidate, no matter whence they come.[22]

Over the years, infringements of academic freedom have resulted from "pressures and attempts to intimidate" brought about by demands for conformity with particular thought patterns in respect of a wide variety of fields, including religion, economics, sociology, politics, sex and literature. Whatever the substance of the demand for conformity, the financial exigencies of modern education have exposed a technique of pressuring and intimidating which poses a grave threat to the independence of universities today: that is, the power of the purse. Harold Howe II, Commissioner of Education in the Johnson Administration has candidly exposed the problem of financial intimidation through the research programs sponsored by the Federal Government.[23] Commissioner Howe asserted, however, that the problem of such intimidation extends beyond governmental intervention, involving private interests of a variety of kinds with some sort of purse-string relationship to the university; "among at least some of these constituencies there is considerable antagonism toward those given to rocking the boat":

The immediate harm of such action is that it entails usurpation of the University's ability to deal with its needs and problems in an objective and effective manner. It inhibits the administration, the faculty, and the student body in working out together procedures, standards, and regulations which, having been commonly developed, will be commonly accepted and followed. The long-range harm is that the threat to withhold support seeks to stifle all dissenters, whatever the merit of their cause, and thereby to induce the campus community to be uninvolved, uncontroversial, unquestioning and uninspiring.[24]

Commissioner Howe affirmed that universities must reject all challenges to academic freedom aided and abetted by financial pressures. Any limitation of the right to conduct free debate and investigation, he asserted, would imperil the freedom of society, not simply the freedom of the university. Commissioner Howe insisted, furthermore, that the constituent elements of the university do not owe the protections of academic freedom merely to noncontroversial subjects and individuals:

. . . Academic freedom is not divisible. You can't have just a comfortable proportion of it or the part of it which produces the ideas you happen to like. You have to keep it whole and complete without compromise, or you don't have it at all. . . .[25]

Commissioner Howe restated, in the clearest terms, the recognized protective commitment of American society, and specifically, the recognized commitment of the various constituencies of any university community—including *trustees, faculty* and *financial sponsors*—to protect academic freedom:

The university community . . . must be free to state its findings and express its judgments. To the extent that it finds established belief to be specious, it must be free to proclaim that finding. To the extent that it finds an unconventional practice potentially beneficial, it must be free to discard convention. And the university must guard the university community's right to do these things.[26]

Within the context of the recognized duty of all universities to protect the working principles of academic freedom against all competing pressures, the academic community of this country has undertaken the task of formulating norms specifying the rights and responsibilities of universities and their faculties in respect of academic freedom. The academic freedom enjoyed by a faculty member assumes his prior duty as a scholar to speak to the truth on issues of importance to his own constituencies. The acceptance of norms of academic responsibility by the American university community must be considered in the light of this recognized responsibility of the professor, which was well summarized in the 1953 AAU Statement:

Timidity must not lead the scholar to stand silent when he ought to speak, particularly in the field of his competence. In matters of conscience and when he has truth to proclaim the scholar has no obligation to be silent in the face of popular disapproval. Some of the great passages in the history of truth have involved the open challenge of popular prejudice in times of tension such as those in which we live.[27]

As a prerequisite to the development of norms of academic responsibility for universities and their faculties, the American university community has attempted to set forth a working definition of the concept of academic freedom.

Professor Arthur Lovejoy, one of the founders of AAUP, proposed the following basic definition:

Academic freedom consists in the absence of, or protection from, such restraints or pressures . . . as are designed to create in the minds of academic scholars (teachers, research workers, and students in publication or in the instruction of students, without interference from political or ecclesiastical authority, or from the administrative officials of the institution in which he is employed, unless his methods are found by qualified bodies of his own profession to be clearly incompetent or contrary to professional ethics.[28]

Professor Fritz Machlup, former President of AAUP, observing that "it is difficult or impossible to formulate an unambiguous definition of academic freedom," offered the following definition:

Academic freedom consists chiefly in the absence of, or protection from, such restraints or pressures . . . as are designed to create in the minds of academic scholars (teachers, research workers, and students) in colleges and universities) fears and anxieties that may inhibit them from freely studying and investigating whatever they are interested in, and from freely discussing, teaching or publishing whatever opinions they have reached.[29]

Although the definitions offered have varied from time to time in phraseology and emphasis, they are all essentially the same in content: "The freedom of professionally qualified persons responsibly to inquire into, discover, interpret, publish and teach the truth as they see it within the fields of their competence . . . without being pressured, penalized, or otherwise molested by authorities or other persons within or without their institutions of learning."[30]

Such definitions as the foregoing cannot reasonably be interpreted as declarations of absolute license or immunity for the college professor; all accepted definitions of academic freedom reflect the responsibilities of the academician which give rise to his rights.

The definitions are limited by their own terms: for example "qualified person"; "responsibly to inquire"; "within their fields of competence." The academic community generally accepts such intrinsic limitations on their freedom, but with, and only with, the express understanding that judgments *applying* those limitations in specific situations must be made *only* by "qualified bodies of [their] own profession," that is, by professional peers.

Nevertheless, pressures (particularly financial) "from without the institution" have worked against the full acceptance of the principle that academic freedom by definition means professional autonomy in self-discipline. Concern among academicians about such pressures stimulated the formation of AAUP in 1915 by a group of prominent faculty members from sixty leading institutions of higher learning. The 1915 Declaration of AAUP's Committee on Academic Freedom and Tenure set the tone for the continuing concern of AAUP with securing observance of basic principles of academic freedom in all universities. AAUP provides a means of vindicating accepted principles of academic responsibility by directing professional attention to academic administrations which have been found to have violated academic freedom, and it has spelled out its policies and decisions on particular cases through the reports of the Committee A on Academic Freedom and Tenure. AAUP has been joined in its efforts by the Association of American Colleges (AAC).

AAUP, in conjunction with AAC, is responsible for the statement of rights and responsibilities pertaining to responsible academic procedure "which is accepted generally throughout the educational world as the most authoritative statement (of the principles of academic freedom)," the 1940 Statement of Principles on Academic Freedom and Tenure.[31] The 1940 Statement has been endorsed by over 50 American educational associations.[32] It is, without question, an *existing,* generally accepted norm of academic freedom and responsibility.

As a norm of academic freedom and responsibility, the 1940 Statement has an identifiable structure, considering in sequence the questions of research, classroom and extramural activity. In the nineteenth century, issues of academic freedom primarily concerned the rights and responsibilities of faculty members in research and scholarly writing, and in classroom teaching. The settled principles applicable to these areas are set forth in Paragraphs (a) and (b) of the 1940 Statement, respectively. In recent decades major pressures (financial and otherwise) to compromise academic freedom have been directed toward the academic freedom of the faculty member as a "citizen" in his conduct with respect to his community. Paragraph (c) of the 1940 Statement sets forth standards for a professor's exercise of his rights of extramural expression as a citizen of his community and concomitantly sets forth the extent of permissible limitations which a university may impose on such expression because of the role in providing recognition of the faculty member concerned. More recently, however, significant "extramural" expressions of faculty members have come to implicate the university institution as a part of the professor's "community." Today, opposition by a citizen-professor to his government's decision to build a certain type of weapons system, for example, may necessarily involve a challenge by the same citizen-professor to the activity of his own university in connection with weapons research. Thus, an extramural (in the sense of extra-classroom) utterance may have intramural effects. This was certainly the case in the dissent at Catholic University, where the professors were taking a public position as to the authority and prerogatives of the University's primary sponsor, the hierarchy of the Roman Catholic Church. Therefore, the 1940 AAUP formulations in Paragraph (c) should be tested anew as guidelines for "extramural" expression in the context of extramural statements with intramural effects and in the context of the tensions that may arise between freedom and loyalty in the university context.

Notes

1. See H. Commager, "The Nature of Academic Freedom," *Saturday Review* 13, 36–37 (August 27, 1966).

2. "The Objectives of The Catholic University of America" (Statement Approved by the Trustees of the University, July 27, 1968), *The Catholic University of America Administrative Bulletin*, Vol. I, No. 1 at 1 (September 3, 1968).

3. *Ibid.*

4. See Article I, *Statutes of the Catholic University of America* (1937; as amended, 1967) (hereinafter "the Statutes").

5. H. Kueng, "Freedom, Intellectual," *The New Catholic Encyclopedia*, Vol. 6 at 100.

6. Developments in the Law—Academic Freedom, 81 *Harv. L. Rev.* 1048 (1968).

7. *Ibid.*

8. R. Fuchs, "Academic Freedom—Its Basic Philosophy, Function, and History," 28 *Law and Contemp. Prob.* 431 (1963) (hereinafter "Fuchs").

9. *Ibid.*

10. 81 *Harv. L. Rev.* 1048 (emphasis supplied).

11. R. Hofstadter & W. Metzger, *The Development of Academic Freedom in the United States* 397, 403 (1955) (hereinafter "Hofstadter & Metzger").

12. *Sweezy v. New Hampshire*, 354 U.S. 234, 250 (1957).

13. *Keyishian v. Bd. of Educ.*, 385 U.S. 589, 603 (1967).

14. 354 U.S. 234, 263 (1957); see generally 81 *Harv L. Rev.* 1048–1105.

15. F. Machlup, "On Some Misconceptions Concerning Academic Freedom," *Academic Freedom and Tenure*, Appendix B, at 177, 180 (L. Joughin ed., 1967), reprinted from 41 *AAUP Bulletin* 753 (Winter 1955) (hereinafter "Machlup").

16. Hofstader & Metzger 405 (emphasis supplied).

17. Machlup 181–82.

18. See D. Fellman, "National Commitment," *Albertus Magnus Guild Bulletin* 5 (December 1968).

19. Association of American Universities, "The Rights and Responsibilities of Universities and Their Faculties" (1962; original publication in 1953) (hereinafter *AAU Statement*).

20. Fuchs 437 .

21. *Ibid.*

22. Machlup 183–184.

23. H. Howe II, "Responsibility and Academic Freedom," Address delivered at Adelphi University Commencement (June 9, 1968) (hereinafter Howe).

24. Howe 4.

25. Howe 5–6.

26. Howe 7.

27. *AAU Statement.*
28. A. Lovejoy, "Academic Freedom," *Encyclopedia of Social Sciences* 384 (1920), cited in W. Murphy, "Academic Freedom—An Emerging Constitutional Right," 28 *Law and Contemp. Prob.* 447, 451n. 11 (1963).
29. Machlup 178.
30. R. Hoffman, "A Note on Academic Freedom," 44 *Phi Delta Kappan* 185 (January 1963).
31. W. Murphy, *supra* note 29, at 451n.11.
32. List of Endorsing Organizations, 53 *AAUP Bulletin* 246 (Spring 1967).

5

The Inquiry:
Accepted Norms
of Extramural Expression

"A faculty member's expression of opinion as a citizen cannot constitute grounds for dismissal unless it clearly demonstrates the faculty member's unfitness for his position. Extramural utterances rarely bear upon the faculty member's fitness for his position."—1964 *Statement on Extramural Utterances, Committee of The American Association of University Professors.*

The controlling principle in AAUP's Paragraph (c) is freedom: when the faculty member speaks or writes extramurally, according to Paragraph (c), "he should be free from institutional censorship and discipline." Paragraph (c) asserts, though, that the position of the faculty member in the community "imposes special obligations." The stated obligations of a faculty member to "be accurate," to "exercise appropriate restraint," to "show respect for the opinions of others" and to "make every effort to indicate that he is not an institutional spokesman" in his public expression are considered to articulate a standard of "academic responsibility."[1] These norms, nearly three decades since their formulation, may appear at first reading to be too vague to be enforceable and indeed unduly restrictive. Why must a professor be *restrained*; what is *appropriate* restraint? Such standards are open to grave abuse, particularly if applied in cases of extramural speech with intramural effects. Why does a professor have *special obligations*; or is

65

the professor to be considered like a lawyer subject to canons of ethics? If so, is the professor to be subject to restrictions on speech only insofar as the speech directly implicates his professional work and competence? AAUP has answered the latter question in the affirmative, clearing the way for a realistic and effective use of the standards in Paragraph (c). The interpretive development of Paragraph (c) by AAUP, moreover, has sharpened the meaning of each of the four standards for faculty expression outside the classroom. It seems clear that, at the very least, AAUP has chosen to interpret the 1940 standards for faculty utterances to limit strictly their disciplinary effects and to emphasize the permissible ambit of public expression which may not be hindered in any way by the University. Furthermore, some debate continues as to whether the norms set forth are not to be read as mere admonitions rather than enforceable standards subject to disciplinary sanction.

From the history of the use of Paragraph (c), it is clear that at most only expressions reflecting on *fitness to teach* may be the subject of any university concern. Committee A of AAUP, which is charged with securing compliance with the principles of academic freedom, approved a Statement on Extramural Utterances in 1964 in an effort to "clarify those sections of the 1940 Statement on Principles of Academic Freedom and Tenure relating to the faculty member's exercise of his freedom of speech as a citizen."[2] The Statement on Extramural Utterances asserts:

> . . . A faculty member's expression of opinion as a citizen cannot constitute grounds for dismissal unless it clearly demonstrates the faculty member's unfitness for his position. Extramural utterances rarely bear upon the faculty member's fitness for his position. Moreover, the final decision should take into account the faculty member's entire record as a teacher and scholar. In the absence of weighty evidence of unfitness, the administration should not prefer charges; and if it is not clearly proved in the hearing that the faculty member is unfit for his position, the faculty committee should make a finding in favor of the faculty member concerned.[3]

In addition, Committee A maintains that "it will view with particular gravity an administrative or board reversal of a favorable faculty committee hearing judgment in a case involving extramural utterances."[4]

Committee A has thus put the academic community on notice that the 1940 Statement in Paragraph (c) states the maximum permissible restraints on the extramural expressions of faculty members, and that, therefore, those restraints will be construed strictly against anyone charging that a faculty member has violated the norms of academic responsibility contained therein. In this connection the Statement on Extramural Utterances specifically referred to an interpretation approved by AAUP and AAC in 1940 of Paragraph (c) of the 1940 Statement, which had articulated the same principle:

If the administration of a college or university feels that a teacher has not observed the admonitions of Paragraph (c) of the section on *Academic Freedom* and believes that the extramural utterances of the teacher may have been such as to raise grave doubts concerning his fitness for his position, it may proceed to file charges. . . . *In pressing such charges the administration should remember that teachers are citizens and should be accorded the freedom of citizens.* In such cases the administration must assume full responsibility and [the AAUP] and [the AAC] are free to make an investigation.[5]

AAUP maintains the practice of investigating and reporting upon alleged infractions of academic freedom as set forth in its statements of principles. AAUP normally acts only upon request of a faculty member who believes that his rights have been infringed. In the event of failure of preliminary negotiations, and if the issue appears deserving of further action, the General Secretary of AAUP appoints an ad hoc Investigating Committee consisting of two or more members of the Association. Upon completion of its investigation the Investigating Committee prepares a report, which is submitted to Committee A for review. After revision by Committee A and the General Secretary, submission to the parties for comment, and possible further revision, the report, giving a detailed account of the facts and an application of AAUP principles to the issues raised, may be published in the *AAUP Bulletin*. This report is the principal statement of the AAUP's position in the case. Committee A then prepares a brief recommendation. The formal action of AAUP, which may involve censure of the offending institution, is taken by resolution adopted at the annual meeting. There is no practice of citing prior cases as precedent. No single tribunal undertakes to develop a systematic statement of principle in the manner of an appellate court. The AAUP reports, together with the action taken by the Association, nonetheless constitute a valuable collection of interpretive decisional material.[6]

Before the Catholic University case, two cases that helped to define the boundaries of university concern with faculty in extramural expression were the *Alabama Polytechnic Institute* case and the *University of Illinois* case (the *Koch* case).

The *Koch* case involved a letter written to the campus newspaper commenting on a prior article dealing with campus sex mores. In his letter Professor Koch criticized the previous article, protested "the widespread crusades against obscenity which are so popular among prudes and puritanical old-maids" and asserted that "college students when faced with this outrageously ignorant code of morality, would seem to me to be acting with remarkable decorum, and surprising meekness, if they do no more than neck at their social functions." The University terminated Professor Koch's contract on the ground that his letter was a breach of responsible academic procedure, particularly in view of the adverse "intramural effect" which the University officials found Professor Koch's views would have on student conduct.[7] In the *Alabama Polytechnic Institute* case, the faculty member had written a letter to the student newspaper criticizing an editorial in that publication dealing with integration of public schools in New York City. The letter included the following statement: "What is difficult to understand is the reasoning of those persons who profess decency, a feeling for their fellow man and who boast of their moral standards, yet who nevertheless hesitate to join the crusade to

drive ignorance, poverty, and social injustice from our midst."
The Board of Trustees refused to renew the subject faculty
member's contract on the ground (among others) that, in view
of the racial tension in Alabama (particularly the then pending
Autherine Lucy case at the University of Alabama) the letter
failed "to exercise appropriate restraint," "to show respect" for
others' opinions and to indicate that the author was not an institutional spokesman.[8] Again, the intramural effects of the statement were critical—the implicit criticism of sponsoring Alabama institutions was a source of the outside objections which
the Trustees heeded.

In the *Alabama Polytechnic Institute* case and in the *Koch* case,
AAUP purposely assumed, in deciding the cases, in favor of the
teachers in question, that the norms of "academic responsibility"
embodied in Paragraph (c) are not merely intended to embody
admonitions to which faculty members "should" adhere, but rather
that they are standards that may be enforced through university
disciplinary sanctions. But whether such restraints can be affirmatively enforced by disciplinary sanction within the University
community remains an open question.[9] The dissenters on the
"jurisdictional" issue in AAUP's final review of the *Koch* case,
for example, agreed with the initial Investigating Committee's
basic judgment that the 1940 Statement of academic responsibility
could not of itself constitute a standard enforceable by dismissal
or suspension or other serious disciplinary action. The following
remarks of one of the dissenters, Professor Warren Taylor, illustrate
the nature of the unsettled dispute.

. . . The Association has never . . . questioned that established
dereliction of duty and professional incompetence are valid tests for
dismissal. These two, singly or in combination, have, in practice, for
the Association, constituted unfitness to teach. . . .
The 1940 Statement of Principles says nothing about a special
standard of "academic responsibility" in a teacher's expression of his
opinion which, when violated, may lead to discipline. It says that
teachers as citizens should be accorded the freedom of citizens. . . . The

1940 Statement sets up no appropriate penalties for inaccuracy, disrespect, or a lack of restraint. It labels its precautions explicitly as "admonitions," not as "standards of discipline." The appended interpretation then spells out a procedure for administrators who believe that a professor's extramural utterances raise doubts concerning his fitness for his position. *For the 1940 Statement to have any consistency at all and freedom from contradiction this can only mean that the teacher's public expression of his opinions may become ground for moving towards his dismissal when and only when those opinions reveal unfitness to teach: what may be established as dereliction of duty and professional incompetence. . .*[10]

In any event, the terms of the 1940 Statement of AAUP as interpreted in the AAUP decisions, have in the relevant cases proved to be a restraining influence on impulses toward discipline and AAUP's emphasis on functional criteria (dereliction of duty, professional incompetence, and, generally, fitness to teach) has served to require that any university discipline of faculty members be related to a deficiency with respect to the work of teaching.

Certain discussions in the report of the Investigating Committees in the *Alabama Polytechnic Institute* case and the *Koch* case[11] are instructive, considered together with other interpretive material, with respect to the *accepted* meaning of the four particular admonitions to the faculty member contained in Paragraph (c): "to be accurate," "to show respect for the opinions of others," "to exercise appropriate restraint" and "to make every effort to indicate that he is not an institutional spokesman."

The Responsibility To Be Accurate

The letter published by Professor Koch in the University newspaper, in the opinion of the Investigating Committee, was an expression of an *opinion,* which some hold to be sound and others do not. The Investigating Committee held that the test of accuracy has no real application in such circumstances.

The test of a controversial theory extends beyond the question of the accuracy of its statement. Copernican astronomy, when first stated, was not accurate in all particulars, but it would have been the height of folly to restrain its public expression for that reason." [12]

As the foregoing commentary indicates, the test of "accuracy" has not been developed as a working criterion of professional responsibility in the sensitive opinion areas most generally implicated in objections to extramural faculty expression. Obviously, however, such offenses as plagiarism, which might be included within the scope of the standard of accuracy, are cognizable within the context of AAUP's norms.

The Responsibility to Exercise Appropriate Restraint

Several of the charges with respect to Professor Koch's letter could be considered under the rubric of "appropriate restraint." The Investigating Committee in the *Koch* case asserted that the professor had the right to express his views not limited by the fact that his publication of them would be prejudicial to the interests of the University in the sense that it would arouse strong protest by alumni, parents or other constituents of the university who disagreed with his position.[13] It considered protection of this right to be fundamental to the existence of academic freedom. This position reflects acceptance of the principle that the trustees owe their protection to faculty members whose legitimate exercise of academic freedom might be challenged by various constituents of the University:

. . . It must be recognized that the academic freedom cannot be measured or limited by vague threats to the welfare of an institution or a community which may or may not result from what a professor says or does. If a professor must hold his tongue lest he cause an alumnus to withhold a gift, a legislator to vote against an appropriation, or student not to register, or a citizen's feelings to be ruffled, he will be free to talk only to himself.[14]

Advisory Letter No. 11 on "Extramural Utterances"[15] confirms the judgment of the Investigating Committees that the "offensive and repugnant" nature of the substance of the views expressed in a communication cannot be an issue under Paragraph (c), and that there is no special obligation on the part of the faculty member "to refrain from extramural utterances that may embarrass the institution in its relationships with the community, alumni, legislature and Board of Trustees":

> [In terms of the standard of appropriate restraint or any other standard of AAUP] neither the error nor the unpopularity of ideas or opinions may provide an adequate basis for such disciplinary action, whatever temporary embarrassment these views may bring to the institution. . . .
>
> It is the view of this Office that the term "appropriate restraint," as used [in Paragraph (c)], refers solely to choice of language and to other aspects of the manner in which a statement is made. It does not refer to the substance of a teacher's remarks.[16]

It is clear that the substance of views expressed cannot be attacked regardless of how embarrassing or offensive such views may be to the various constituencies to which any university owes its allegiance. Nor may a charge of breach of academic responsibility for lack of appropriate restraint be based on a contention that the statement was not reasoned or reasonable; the Investigating Committee in the *Koch* case expressed a key insight into the meaning of the phrase "responsible academic procedure" with respect to extramural expression of views:

> In any case, it is difficult to see how the question of the reasonableness of the view is related to the question of a person's freedom to express it. Clearly Professor Koch related the views to which he gave expression, and the letter gives every indication *that he stood ready to discuss at length the evidential merits of his position.*[17]

At the very most, a university may require only that a faculty member's public expression be "supportable." Moreover, even this requirement may be dangerously close to an impermissible attack on the substance of expression.

It is clear that according to AAUP sources, "appropriate restraint" concerns choice of language and other aspects of the manner of an expression. Advisory Letter No. 11 limits the scope of inquiry with respect to manner, however: "[Appropriate restraint] does not refer to the *times* and *place* of [the faculty member's] utterance."[18]

In terms of "choice of language," the consideration by the Investigating Committee in the *Koch* case of various claims that the "language and tone" of Professor Koch's letter were "inappropriate" is particularly significant. The Investigating Committee found that the mere claim that Professor Koch's letter employed techniques of "overstatement and ridicule" was not sufficient to show a violation of AAUP standards of responsible academic procedure. The Investigating Committee also dismissed a general charge that Professor Koch's letter was not in keeping with proper standards of "temperateness" and "dignity," since the standards of responsibility, applied in this way, would make many of the more colorful and indeed educationally effective academicians subject to discipline, leaving the field to the dull and the innocuous.[19] The AAUP report in the *Alabama Polytechnic* case similarly concluded that "academic freedom does not exist to protect only dry detailing of facts, and professors must have leeway to speak with vigor and conviction."[20]

Finally, the Investigating Committee in the *Koch* case rejected the argument that the expression of Professor Koch was inappropriate because it constituted "incitement to misconduct":

Every forceful expression of an idea is an encouragement to act upon it. As Justice Holmes has said, "Every idea is an incitement." To say that a faculty member may express unorthodox ideas, but is violating academic responsibility if his ideas encourage action, renders the right of expression meaningless. Perhaps a line must be drawn somewhere, although we do not see any satisfactory way of drawing it short of the point where expression becomes an illegal solicitation to crime, a point certainly not reached here. But the prohibition surely cannot extend to everything which falls within the term "encouragement" or "espousal." [21]

The Responsibility to Show Respect for the Opinions of Others

The Ad Hoc Committee's consideration of the charge that Professor Koch did not show respect for the opinions of others illustrates particular sensitivity to the uncertain boundary separating failure to show such respect from failure to hold substantively "acceptable" views:

> The next objection is that Professor Koch "castigated those who might disagree with his conclusions as outrageously ignorant," and thus failed to show "respect for the opinions of others." But Professor Koch's disagreement with the opinions held by others does not seem to be of any different scale or temper from what one frequently finds expressed in public controversy and often academic controversy. . . . The implication seems clear enough that in this conclusion also the Board intrinsically appeals to the unacceptability of the ideas themselves, not to Professor Koch's supposedly intemperate manner of expressing them.[22]

The Responsibility to Make Every Effort to Indicate that He Is Not an Institutional Spokesman

The Illinois Trustees charged Professor Koch with violating his responsibility to disassociate himself from the University because he included his academic title at the University with his signature on the published letter.[23] The same charge was made in the *Alabama Polytechnic Institute* case.[24] The Investigating Committees rejected these contentions.[25]

The Investigating Committee in *Koch* stated, in its discussion of whether the standards of "academic responsibility" stated in Paragraph (c) were subject to disciplinary sanction, that:

> It is true that a faculty member can never completely dissociate himself from the institution to which he belongs. *Nevertheless, it is*

also true that the community now recognizes, or can be educated to recognize, that expressions of individual faculty members on controversial public issues are not to be attributed to the University.[26]

It seems clear from the reports of the AAUP Investigating Committees that the obligation to make every effort to indicate that one is not an institutional spokesman does not impose responsibility to speak anonymously, or to avoid disclosing for identification purposes one's academic background. Given the common understanding that individual views of faculty members, identified as such, are a fortiori not the views of their institutions, it seems clear that AAUP requires of responsible professors only that they avoid *creating the impression* that they are speaking for their universities, by indicating that they are speaking as individuals; they need not explicitly deny that they are institutional spokesmen.[27]

Indeed, the emphasized words are the very ones used to express this responsibility in AAUP's 1966 Statement on Professional Ethics. Other Statements with respect to general norms of academic freedom have been put forward since AAUP's 1940 Statement. During the period of the McCarthy influence in 1953, the chief administrative officers of 37 universities comprising the membership of AAU (including The Catholic University of America) adopted a Statement on "The Rights and Responsibilities of the Universities and Their Faculties."[28] The AAU Statement stated general principles relating to the obligations and responsibilities of university faculties. Those stated obligations may be summarized as the following:

1) to observe lawful limits in his speech, writing or other action (law in this instance refers to the civil law);

2) to weigh the validity of his opinions and the manner in which they are expressed so as to avoid ill-advised (though not necessarily illegal) public acts or other instances which may do serious harm to his profession, his university, to education and to the general welfare;

3) to refrain from engaging in any kind of clandestine or con-

spiratorial activities that would compromise his candor and integrity;

4) to speak with candor to public authorities when called upon to answer for his convictions.[29]

The foregoing norms are obviously far more restrictive of academic freedom than the generally accepted principles laid down by AAUP in the 1940 Statement, as interpreted, and must be construed in the light of the more general acceptance in the academic community as a whole of the AAUP formulations.[30]

The AAU Statement apparently attempts to articulate a disciplinary standard of "academic integrity"—the Statement refers to the establishment of university tribunals to judge the nature and degree of any "trespass upon academic integrity"—but the AAU Statement does not make explicit whether violations of academic integrity are grounds for dismissal in themselves or only relevant evidence on the broader issue of academic fitness.

The injunctions forbidding unlawful or clandestine activities and requiring candor with public authorities must be read in the light of then contemporaneous national concern with internal security. Passing over these matters, the surviving injunction of the AAU Statement is the injunction against ill-advised public acts or utterances that may do serious harm to the profession, university, education in general or to the general welfare. This limitation, along with the injunction to "weigh the *validity* of his opinions and the manner in which they are expressed" could, if applied, effectively negate any working notion of academic freedom. The injunction against "ill-advised acts" is utterly vague (ill-advised from the point of view of a university's fund-raising activities? ill-advised from the point of view of the faculty member's career?); if it is to have any legitimate meaning, it must take its content from the accepted notion of responsibility articulated in the 1940 Statement and its interpretation. Those interpretations have, furthermore, clearly indicated that the substance (the *validity*) of opinion may not be called into question under the "appropriate restraint" (or any other) clause of AAUP (unless the statement manifests an in-

competence indicating grave reason to question fitness to teach)
and that inquiries regarding *manner* of expression should not concern the time and place of expression.[31]

The AAU Statement does not express any standard specifically comparable with AAUP's injunctions to show respect for
the opinion of others and to make every effort to avoid identification with the university, but the AAU Statement implicitly acknowledges the common understanding that faculty members expressing
their individual opinions are presumed not to be speaking for the
university: "Historically the word 'university' is a guarantee of
standards. It implies endorsement not of its members' views but
of their capability and integrity."[32]

It is at least clear that a notion that a faculty member must not
speak unless he can guarantee that his views will not be identified
as the views of the university finds no support in the AAU Statement.

The AAU Statement, insofar as it is to be considered an *accepted* norm of responsible academic procedure, must be interpreted and construed in the light of the 1940 Statement of AAUP
and subsequent interpretations of that AAUP Statement. No additional norms are set forth in the AAU Statement that are not
either contained by implication in the 1940 Statement or, indeed,
refuted and rejected expressly by the 1940 Statement and the
subsequent interpretations of the 1940 Statement.

A Statement issued by the American Civil Liberties Union
(ACLU) in 1956, and reissued in 1960, entitled "Academic Freedom and Academic Responsibility," asserts that ACLU is prepared to intervene in appropriate cases if administrative action
is taken against a teacher absent a prior unfavorable faculty judgment based on "professional incompetence," "perversion of academic process" or "immoral conduct."[33] The ACLU Statement also
reflects the context of "internal security" controversy. The criterion of "immoral conduct" is vague and, of course, irrelevant to
the Inquiry at Catholic University. The other grounds for dismissal approved by ACLU parallel the "dereliction of duty" and

"manifest incompetence" formulations which AAUP has used to describe the general offenses cognizable under the question "fitness to teach."

With respect to the freedom of faculty members *as citizens,* the ACLU Statement proposes that:

> Outside the academic scene the teacher has no less freedom than other citizens. He is not required because of his profession to maintain a timorous silence as a price of professional status. On the contrary, his greater knowledge imposes upon him the two-fold duty of advancing new and useful ideas and of helping to bury ideas which are outworn. However, since the public may judge his profession and his institution by his utterances, he should make every effort to maintain high professional excellence and at the same time to indicate that he does not speak for the institution which employs him. When he speaks or writes as an individual he should be free from both institutional and public censorship or discipline.[34]

The ACLU Statement, insofar as it directly addresses the problem of extramural expression, generally reflects the basic concerns that are found in Paragraph (c) of the 1940 Statement of AAUP. The admonition to make every effort to maintain professional standards in public writing and speaking reflects AAUP's more specific concerns with accuracy, appropriate restraint and respect for opinions of others. The basic position of ACLU, interpreted in the light of the accepted specifications of AAUP, seems to be that a faculty member has the same rights as any other citizen subject to the qualification that when he speaks or writes publicly, he should make clear that he does not speak for his institution (by making clear that he is speaking as an individual).

Of all of the foregoing statements of norms, the AAUP standards are the most generally recognized in American universities, and, indeed, incorporate the best elements of the other proposed standards. The Trustees of Catholic University, who on September 5, questioned the declarations and actions of the dissenting professors under *accepted norms of academic freedom and responsible academic procedure,* as well as under the professors' obligations to the University as specified in its Statutes by their responsibilities as Roman Catholic theologians, thereby focused the Inquiry around the standards of AAUP. The latter two particular areas of responsibility may be analyzed in terms of "dereliction of duty" and "professional incompetence," respectively, recognized by AAUP as the sole possible bases for university disciplinary action against faculty members. The first area of responsibility concerns the stated AAUP norms of responsible academic procedure in "extramural utterances." Moreover, it is clear that any institution considering charges against a professor for violation of the norms for public expression outlined in Paragraph (c) of the 1940 Statement of AAUP must answer *two* questions affirmatively before subjecting him to inquisition for his extramural conduct: (1) whether there are reasonable grounds to believe that the subject professor has violated any of the four admonitions of the 1940 Statement respecting extramural utterances, as interpreted in subsequent AAUP statements and opinions, *and* (2) if so, whether such violation amounts to dereliction of duty or professional incompetence giving grave reason to question the fitness of the particular individual to teach.

The presentations on the foregoing areas of responsibility submitted to the Inquiry Board by the subject professors through their counsel (and reiterated with some summarization, in the foregoing chapters) were supplemented by testimony of distinguished "expert" witnesses. Dr. Robert Cross, who was then President of Hunter College of the City of New York and is now President of Swarthmore College, was the key witness on the norms of expression.

President Cross testified as a general matter that, contrary to the Catholic University Trustees' press release, the declarations and actions of the subject professors respecting the Encyclical raised no serious questions in his understanding of the norms of responsible academic procedure, which understanding was basically the same as set forth by the subject professors in their written testimony and reiterated in this chapter.

Further exploration of the specific standards set forth by AAUP continued with President Cross and other witnesses in the Inquiry.

On the basis of the interpretive data presented "the responsibility to be accurate" was understood in the Inquiry as a requirement of candor to the effect that a professor speaking or writing publicly should properly identify opinion as opinion and fact as fact, and must avoid deliberate falsehood such as distorting the opinions of others or adopting them as his own without due acknowledgment.

As to questions of "accuracy", all the participants in the Inquiry understood that the conduct called into question by the Trustees was a dissenting *opinion* of Roman Catholic theologians. The question of whether the Statement represented a "supportable" scholarly position, a question sometimes associated with the standard of "accuracy," but more directly related to the question of professional competence, was indeed raised by the Trustees on September 5. That question of the "supportability" of the theologians' dissent within Roman Catholic theology is treated in chapter seven, which deals with issues of professional competence. Expert theological testimony on this question was presented by the subject professors themselves and by distinguished outside experts.

On the basis of the interpretive data presented, the "responsibility to show respect for the opinions of others" was understood in the Inquiry to require, in conjunction with the standard of accuracy, that the professor speaking or writing publicly not distort the opinions of others or adopt them as his own without due acknowledgement, and requires an acknowledgment that contrary opinion exists and the accurate substantive description of it if description is offered. The duty to show respect for the opinions of others does not require the professor speaking or writing publicly to refrain from criticism of those who hold contrary opinions; the temper of such criticism is to be judged according to the tenor of similar expressions by other academicians in similar circumstances, which would indicate the customary limits of such criticism.

With respect to the AAUP norm requiring "respect for the opinions of others," then, it did not seem to any of the expert witnesses testifying in the course of the Inquiry that the subject professors' declarations and actions had failed to show proper regard for the person of the Pope as the Trustees suggested; in fact, none of the participants in the Inquiry could find any meaningful basis whatsoever for the charge, forwarded in the Trustees' December 23 letter, that there was some question about the professors' respect for the Pope.

On the basis of the interpretive data presented, "the responsibility to exercise appropriate restraint" was understood in the Inquiry to refer solely to choice of language and other aspects of the manner in which a statement is made, and not to refer to the substance of a teacher's extramural expression. Thus, it is not a violation of the duty of appropriate restraint merely to express publicly a controversial opinion, and the standard of appropriate restraint cannot be used to impose subjective or even institutional concepts of "good taste" or the like. Nor may "controversial" utterances be questioned; indeed, the very *controversy* about certain views would suggest that such views are a fortiori "supportable." Appropriate restraint does not refer to the times and places of expression: "where" and "when" an expression occurs are not issues under the duty of appropriate restraint. Appropriate restraint requires that the choice of language and the manner of public expression (excluding considerations of time and place) should not exceed the customary limits of professional propriety, as such limits are indicated by similar expressions by other academicians in similar circumstances.

President Theodore M. Hesburgh, of the University of Notre Dame and Chairman of the United States Civil Rights Commission, also addressed himself, in written testimony submitted to the Inquiry Board, to AAUP's norm of "appropriate restraint" in extramural expression. In this regard, he observed that the public Statement of dissent subscribed to by the subject professors was not a violation: "It seems that any other manner of response would have been virtually impossible. It was an emergency situation. The Encyclical and comments on it were in the public press. The press immediately sought out the theologians. . . . President

Hesburgh was further of the opinion that "under the circumstances, they were virtually compelled to some sort of honest response. The alternative would have been to hide or to issue a series of ambiguous 'no comments' or to have issued dishonest statements of compliance."

On the basis of the interpretive data presented, the "responsibility to make every effort to indicate that one is not an institutional spokesman" was understood in the Inquiry to be conditioned in practice by the common presumption that when a faculty member indicates that he is expressing himself publicly in *his individual capacity,* he is to be understood as not speaking for his university. Thus the requirement of dissociation was understood as a requirement to make every effort necessary in the circumstances to indicate that one is not an institutional spokesman. President Hesburgh, in this respect, called the Inquiry Board's attention to the *Notre Dame Faculty Manual,* which, in adopting the substance of AAUP's 1940 Statement, requires not "every effort" but "every reasonable effort." President Cross took the same position in his oral testimony. Thus the faculty member is not required to refrain from identifying himself as a professor at a particular university when he expresses himself publicly—in fact, the norms of academic freedom and responsibility expressly permit the faculty member to so identify himself without violating his responsibility to indicate that he is not an institutional spokesman. As a rule, a faculty member is not required expressly to deny that he is an institutional spokesman so long as he makes clear that his use of his academic title is for identification purposes only. But AAUP clearly does not require the faculty member to *guarantee* that his public expression will not be interpreted as an official university pronouncement; such a rule would mean that a faculty member would speak publicly at the peril of innocent or unreasonable confusion on the part of one or more persons or constituencies of the university.

President Cross found no basis in the professors' actions for any questions, let alone charges, as to violations of the norm of extramural expression requiring dissociation from the University. Indeed, all the expert witnesses who testified before the Inquiry

Board were asked whether there was any impression in their minds that the subject professors had failed to disassociate themselves from the University in their Statement, as required by AAUP's norm. None of the witnesses saw any question raised by the professors' actions in respect of that norm. President Hesburgh, in his written testimony submitted to the Inquiry Board, affirmed that the subject professors had in fact "fully satisfied" the AAUP norm requiring disassociation, particularly because the spokesman for the subscribers had made clear that the institutions of the subscribers to the Statement of dissent were released to the press solely for identification purposes.

Finally, since extramural expressions, including those with intramural effects such as the *Koch* and *Alabama Polytechnic* incidents, rarely bear upon a faculty member's fitness for his position, it was understood in the Inquiry that violation of any or all of the responsibilities set forth in Paragraph (c) do not necessarily give reason to question the fitness of the faculty member to teach. To constitute reason to question fitness to teach, alleged violations of the responsibilities set forth in Paragraph (c) must appear to constitute dereliction of duty or professional incompetence. Proceedings leading to dismissal should not be preferred absent weighty evidence of such unfitness to teach; and a finding of unfitness to teach requires clear proof in the record. In cases involving extramural faculty expression with intramural effects, a university bears a heavy burden of self-justification if it attempts to discipline or otherwise restrict faculty members on account of their public utterances.

Notes

1. T. Emerson & D. Haber, "Academic Freedom of the Faculty Member as Citizen," 28 *Law & Contemp. Prob.* 525, 528 (1963) (hereinafter "Emerson & Haber").
2. Introduction to *1964 Committee A Statement on Extramural Utterances,* reprinted in *Academic Freedom and Tenure* 64 (L. Joughin, ed., 1967) hereinafter "Statement on Extramural Utterances").
3. *Id.* at 64–65.

4. *Id.* at 65.
5. "Interpretation" of 1940 Statement," reprinted in *Academic Freedom and Tenure* 39 (L. Joughin, ed., 1967) (emphasis supplied).
6. See generally Emerson & Haber 534–36.
7. 49 *AAUP Bulletin* 25 (Spring, 1963).
8. 44 *AAUP Bulletin* 158 (Spring, 1958).
9. See Emerson & Haber 528.
10. 49 *AAUP Bulletin* at 42–43 (emphasis supplied).
11. Although the Investigating Committee in the Koch case was of the opinion that the standard of "academic responsibility" is not a valid basis for reprimand, dismissal or other official discipline, the Committee nevertheless offered certain interpretations of the meaning of academic responsibility which take on significance in the light of Committee A's view that the standard of academic responsibility set forth in Paragraph (c) is *enforceable* by University action (although Committee A decided the case on procedural grounds).
12. 49 *AAUP Bulletin* at 39.
13. *Id.* at 35.
14. 44 *AAUP Bulletin* at 168.
15. Advisory letters are issued by the Washington Office staff of AAUP to answer questions from members about established Association policy. Committee A has authorized from time to time publication of selected excerpts from Advisory Letters in the *AAUP Bulletin*.
16. *Academic Freedom and Tenure* 132, 134 (L. Joughin, ed., 1967), reprinted from 49 *AAUP Bulletin* 393 (Winter, 1963) (emphasis supplied).
17. 49 *AAUP Bulletin* at 38–39 (emphasis supplied).
18. *Academic Freedom and Tenure* 132 (emphasis supplied).
19. 49 *AAUP Bulletin* at 39.
20. 44 *AAUP Bulletin* at 167.
21. 49 *AAUP Bulletin* at 38.
22. *Id.* at 39.
23. *Ibid.*
24. 44 *AAUP Bulletin* at 161.
25. 49 *AAUP Bulletin* at 39; 44 *AAUP Bulletin* at 167.
26. 49 *AAUP Bulletin* at 37 (emphasis supplied).
27. See AAUP Statement on Professional Ethics, 52 *AAUP Bulletin* 290–91 (Autumn, 1966), especially part V: "When he speaks or acts as a private person [the professor] avoids creating the impression that he speaks or acts for his college or university." See also 44 *AAUP Bulletin* at 167.
28. Statement of the Academic Freedom Committee of the American Civil Liberties Union (ACLU), issued in 1958, criticizes the AAU

Statement as implying "an authorization it did not in fact possess," pointing out that the signatories to the AAU Statement were acting as individuals and not as representatives of the considered views of the trustees or faculties of their respective institutions. Emerson and Haber, 530 n.7, citing "Statement of the Academic Freedom Committee of the ACLU on the 1953 Statement of the AAU" (March, 1958).

29. AAU Statement; the further assertion that invocation of the Fifth Amendment is grounds for questioning fitness to teach is not treated.

30. The AAU Statement apparently, in its time, was hailed as a liberal presentation of the issues and did much to curb the excess of the Joseph McCarthy era. Emerson & Haber 532.

31. See pp. II–23 to II–25 *supra*.

32. AAU Statement.

33. 42 *AAUP Bulletin* 517 (Winter, 1956).

34. Id. at 518.

6

The Inquiry:
Existing Norms
of Academic Freedom
in Church-Related Schools

*"No confessional standard obviates the requirement for responsible liberty of conscience in the Christian community and the practice of the highest ideals of academic freedom."—
American Association of Theological Schools, "Academic Freedom and Tenure in the Theological School" (1960).*

The 1940 Statement of AAUP, in Paragraph (b), states that "limitations of academic freedom because of religious or other aims of the institution should be clearly stated in writing at the time of the appointment." At the 1965 Annual Meeting of AAUP, a "Special Committee on Academic Freedom in Church-Related Institutions" was appointed to "study and make more explicit the meaning of the 1940 Statement of Principles on Academic Freedom and Tenure vis-à-vis church-related institutions."[1] The Special Committee reviewed the written regulations and policies of nearly 200 church-related colleges and universities (and, less formally, the practices of some of them), considered the kinds of academic freedom issues which have arisen in such institutions and sought the guidance of a limited number of knowledgeable persons within and outside the Association. In its Report, the Special Committee recalled that AAUP "has insisted that any re-

strictions on the academic freedom of faculties in church-related
or proprietary institutions be directly related to institutional aims,
and that they be published. And it has noted that each restriction
might diminish the institution's academic effectiveness and standing."[2] The Report asserted that the reference in the 1940 Statement to special limitations on academic freedom in church-related
schools should not be construed as an invitation to impose such
restrictions and should not give rise to the implication "that the
adoption of religious purposes necessitates different standards or
conditions of freedom."[3]

The Report warned that " 'At some point in the scale of self-
imposed restrictions a college or university that comes under them
may, of course, cease to be an institution of higher education
according to the prevailing conception.' "[4]

The foregoing remarks preface the the Draft Statement on
Academic Freedom in Church-related Colleges and Universities
promulgated by the Special Committee. The Draft Statement recommends:

> Any limitation on academic freedom should be essential to the
> religious aims of the institution, and should be imposed only after
> consultation among faculty, administration, and governing body. Stu-
> dent opinion on such limitation also would be helpful.
>
> Such limitation with its supporting rationale and relevance to the
> institution's educational objectives should be clearly stated in writing
> with reasonable particularity and made a matter of public knowledge.
> A copy of this statement should be provided to prospective teachers
> at the beginning of negotiations for appointment.
>
> The faculty member should respect the stated aims of an institution
> to which he accepts an appointment, but *academic freedom protects
> his right to express, clarify, and interpret positions—including those
> identified as his own—which are divergent from those of the institu-
> tion and of the church which supports it.*[5]

The emphasized portion of the foregoing Recommendation con-
fronts most bluntly the problem of extramural statements with intramural effects. However, the Report and Recommendation continue AAUP's toleration of special limitations in the classroom

situation. Although the subject conduct at Catholic University was clearly extramural (in the sense that it was *nonclassroom* expression) and thus not subject to any recognized "special limitation," it is apparent that the same interests which provoke demands for institutional loyalty in the classroom invite similar demands relating to extramural expressions which have intramural effect. Conclusions respecting such "extramural expression with intramural effects" as the Catholic University dissent, therefore, could have an important bearing on the continued advisability of permitting "special limitations" on classroom teaching. AAUP interpretive opinion respecting the exercise of academic freedom on church-related campuses has certainly moved at least to the boundaries suggested by the Draft Statement, and some of the reported cases suggest that academic tolerance of special limits on classroom expression related to religious purposes is wearing thin. Some church-related institutions, moreover, have rejected any limitations of academic freedom, whether in research, in the classroom or in "extramural" speech. Such affirmations of academic freedom and autonomy are consistent with the trend of AAUP case studies in the field.

In the *Caldwell* case a professor was suspended and then dismissed because his marriage outside the Catholic Church to a student at a nearby college was said to have given "scandal" and thus to constitute a breach of his contract.[6] It was common knowledge before the wedding that Mr. Caldwell considered that he was no longer a Catholic. The charge of giving scandal was considered to be a substantive violation of academic freedom by the AAUP Investigating Committee:

The dismissal of a faculty member and the abrogation of his contract because of "scandal" are not justifiable under any acceptable academic standard. This is true if for no other reason than, as becomes clear from the facts in the case at hand, that *the charge of "scandal" is not susceptible to common and specific definition. To the President of Saint Mary's College and to some others, it meant bad public example. To others it meant inaccurate or volatile or ambiguous dis-*

course. To still others it meant bad publicity. It meant everything and it meant nothing. Faced with such a protean charge, it was all but impossible for the defendant to know what he was defending himself against.[7]

The Investigating Committee made clear that the *image* of an institution or its desire to avoid "embarrassment" vis-à-vis one or more of its constituencies is not grounds, even in a Church-sponsored institution, for compromising the principles of academic freedom with respect to extramural activities:

When the President, the faculty hearing committee, and the Board of Trustees considered the 1940 *Statement of Principles on Academic Freedom and Tenure, it appears that they focused upon those portions dealing with a professor's responsibilities and used these in conjunction with minor indiscretions to justify dismissal. A more relevant portion of the Statement was neglected: "The college or university teacher is a citizen, a member of a learned profession and an officer of an educational institution. When he speaks or writes as a citizen, he should be free from institutional censorship or discipline."* Mr. Caldwell was not granted the freedom accorded a citizen to be what he is and to live as he believes. He was dismissed for acting in what was regarded by some as an unconventional way, even when his unconventionality had been known to some and had not been hidden from others. *His academic reputation and his contractual rights were sacrificed for the sake of the public image of the institution.* The responsibility for the wrong done to Mr. Caldwell may be fairly shared by the faculty, the administration, and the Board of Trustees of the College.[8]

The *Caldwell* case confirms that AAUP's toleration of special limitations on academic freedom applicable in Church-related schools extends only to special limitations applied to *classroom* conduct of the teacher. In the 1940 Statement, mention of such special limitations is made *only* in Paragraph (b), which deals with the academic freedom of the teacher in the classroom; no mention of the permissibility of such special limitations is made in Paragraph (a), which deals with the writing and research freedom of faculty members, nor is any mention of special limitations made in Paragraph (c), which concerns the freedom of professors in their extramural conduct, whether or not such conduct is related to professional endeavors. Professor Caldwell's university had asserted that "scandalous" extramural activity was impermissible. The Investigating Committee characterized such charges as hopelessly vague, but its more fundamental criticism was that such special limitations, having their source in the religious sponsorship of the institution, could not restrict the freedom of the faculty member in his extramural conduct. The *Caldwell* case, and the rationale behind it (indeed, the case involved "conduct" rather than "utterance" in the strict sense), together with a comparison of Paragraphs (a), (b) and (c) of the 1940 Statement, makes clear that the assertion in Paragraph (c) that a teacher speaking or writing in an extramural forum should be free from institutional censorship or discipline applies undiluted even by any otherwise tolerated "special limitation" in Church-related schools.

Other cases give further evidence that AAUP insists that such special limitations must not interfere with extramural expression.

In the *Shelton* case[9] the contract of Professor Austin J. Shelton, Jr., was terminated on one day's telegraphic notice by Mercy College. The AAUP Investigating Committee study revealed that one basic "cause" of the dismissal notice was the adverse reaction by unnamed "constituents" of the college to the publication and publicization of a book by Dr. Shelton. "Constituents of the College read the book, disapproved of it, and brought their unfavorable opinions to the attention of Sister Mary Lucille," the College President.[10] She informed Professor Shelton that she "had to have some answers to the criticisms [she] was encountering from many of our constituents."[11] She commissioned a critique of Professor Shelton's book by a professor at another university; in part on basis of that critique, the College then terminated Professor Shelton's contract.

Although the Investigation Committee report on the Mercy College case stressed its criticism of the procedural deficiencies involved in the dismissal of Dr. Shelton, the Investigating Committee made significant comments about the relationship of the Church-related school (or any school, for that matter) with its "constituents." The initial notice of termination had stated:

. . . There is undeniable evidence that you are not representative of either the goals or spirit of a Catholic college. As an individual you can claim a personal freedom that is no concern of ours but we have a responsibility and a right to demand conformity to the traditions, ideals, and the spirit of a college maintained and supported by the Sisters of Mercy. *You are the occasion of a severe censure of the College.* This forces our action.[12]

In this context and in view of the complaints of various unnamed "constituents" AAUP's Investigating Committee concluded:

. . . The imputations respecting [Professor Shelton's] nonconformity to the goals, traditions, ideals, and spirit of a Catholic college are so vague and so fraught with subjective content that they cannot be viewed as constituting a statement of adequate cause for termination. *To say further that a faculty member has brought even "severe censure" to his college lays no better grounds for his separation. Indeed, as a member of the academic community of higher education in the United States and therefore sharing the goals, traditions, ideals, and spirit of that community, it is the duty of a college or university to withstand and to defend itself against "censure" by its "constituency" when the cause of the criticism is the responsible exercise of academic freedom by members of its faculty.*[13]

In the *Tench* case, Professor Richard T. Tench, a member of the faculty of the Gonzaga University School of Law, received a notice of nonrenewal under circumstances which led the Investigating Committee of AAUP to conclude that his academic procedural and tenure rights had been violated.[14] In the context of its discussion of those rights, the Investigating Committee made the following comments concerning some of the substantive bases for summary dismissal invoked by Gonzaga University under the

Church-related schools clause of Paragraph (b) of the 1940 Statement.

Concerning the ground of "grave offense against Catholic doctrine or morality," the Investigating Committee observed that:

> . . . The 1940 Statement of Principles on Academic Freedom and
> Tenure recognizes the propriety of limitations, suitably indicated, on
> academic freedom because of the religious aims of an institution. Just
> how specific and what form generally the written exposition of such
> limitations should be or take admittedly is a complex matter in regard
> to which institutions are entitled to some flexibility in approach and
> treatment. The committee is convinced, however, that the statement
> [of the above ground for summary dismissal], commendable as it is
> for its candor and forthright statement of position, is not the appropri-
> ate way for handling a matter as important and complex as this.
> It is to be noted that the concern of the committee relates to the
> substantive as well as the procedural aspects and implications of such
> a provision.[15]

It is clear, moreover, that Church-sponsored universities, like
universities generally, are subject to financial pressures to compromise responsible academic procedure in order to please one or
another constituency.

> In the midst of their efforts to secure stronger financial support for
> their schools many administrators of church related colleges are con-
> fronted with representatives of their own religious groups who not
> only fail to provide even meager support to the financial needs of their
> colleges but actually seek to undermine the support given to such
> schools through their negative criticisms and obstructive tactics.[16]

The principles expressed by the Investigating Committee and
other AAUP authorities, together with the Report and Recommendations of the Special Committee of AAUP on Academic
Freedom in Church-related Schools, are clear indications of developing notions of academic responsibility as they apply to Church-
related universities and faculties. Those notions are that any limitations on academic freedom in Church-related schools will be

strictly construed to preclude restricting the freedom of faculty members as citizens; that faculty members must have written notice at the time of appointment of any restriction to be applied, and that such restrictions, even in writing, must embody specific, understandable standards and not ambiguous and amorphous ones; that the rationale of any such restrictions must be a matter of public record available to the subject professors;[17] that embarrassment of various sponsoring constituents of the university is not sufficient cause for limiting academic freedom; and, specifically, that AAUP is prepared to protect a faculty member who is fired, terminated or disciplined merely because he expresses opinions offensive to Church constituencies of his university.

AAUP has stressed that "special limitations" must be related to *fundamental* purposes and must be properly administered from a procedural point of view, through its requirement for *written* notice in advance of any limitations to be applied and its assertion that written notice "is intended to insure exactness of understanding so that the teacher will know as well as he can what he may do and what he may not do with respect to *certain areas of his teaching* which touch on the religious concerns of the institution. . . ."[18]

President Cross of Hunter College, in his expert testimony before the Inquiry Board, affirmed that in his opinion AAUP's tolerance of "special limitations" on academic freedom in Church-related schools was inapplicable to extramural expression, such as the subject professors' dissent.

While AAUP apparently to date permits a Church-related university to carve out an area of *classroom* inculcation in particular subject matters which may be subject to the prescriptions of Church-related institutions without sanction from the academic community, at the same time, AAUP has taken a firm stand protective of the academic freedom of *all* college professors in their extramural conduct, even when such conduct has what the school may consider to be adverse intramural effect. To the extent that a Church-related school applies special limitations to such extramural conduct of faculty members, to that same extent it is understood in the academic world to approach or, indeed, reach that "point in the scale of self-imposed restrictions at which a college may cease to be an institution of higher education according to the prevailing conception." However the presence of a *theology* curriculum need not prevent an institution from rightfully claiming to be an institution of higher learning "according to the prevailing conception." The generally accepted norms of academic freedom and responsible procedure developed in the centers of American theological study (the most "Church-related" of all Church-related schools) evidence a strong commitment to academic freedom consistent with the trend of AAUP opinion regarding Church-related schools. The American Association of Theological Schools (AATS) has given serious consideration to the problem of how believing Christians reconcile the tenets of their religious faith with the demands of scholarly investigation, both speculative and pastoral. The AATS Statement, "Academic Freedom and Tenure in the Theological School," first issued in 1960, provides an experienced judgment concerning the existing norms of pursuit and communication of theological truth.[19] The prefatory remarks in the AATS Statement show a Christian concern for the principles of academic freedom:

The Christian faith directs all thought and life toward God who is the source of truth, the judge of all human thoughts, and the ultimate end of all theological inquiry.

The freedom of the Christian . . . is never the freedom merely to be left alone or to ignore basic obligations.

The concept of freedom appropriate to theological schools will respect . . . confessional loyalty, both in the institutions and their individual members. At the same time, no confessional standard obviates the requirement for responsible liberty of conscience in the Christian community and the practice of the highest ideals of academic freedom.[20]

The first principle of academic freedom enunciated by AATS is clearly in harmony with the general understanding of scholarly endeavor:

The theological teacher and his students have the inquiry for truth central to their vocation and they are free to pursue this inquiry.[21]

The AATS Statement reflects the basic principles articulated by AAUP in the 1940 Statement and subsequent interpretations of that Statement as applicable norms of responsible theological procedure.

The AATS assertion that any requirement for subscription to a confessional or doctrinal standard "should be mutually understood at the time of [the theology professor's] affiliation with the institution"[22] clearly parallels AAUP's insistence in both the 1940 Statement and the 1967 recommendations concerning Church-related schools that limitations of academic freedom because of religious aims of the institution "should be clearly stated in writing at the time of the appointment."[23]

The AATS assertion that the theology professor "should have freedom in the classroom to discuss his subject in which he has competence and may claim to be a specialist without harassment or limitations"[24] is basically the equivalent of the assertion in the 1940 Statement that "the teacher is entitled to freedom in the classroom to discuss his subject . . . [excepting] controversial matter not related to his subject."[25]

With respect to extramural utterances, AATS clearly expresses the same concept of freedom set forth by AAUP in Paragraph (c) of the 1940 Statement:

The teacher should be free to express and act upon his conscientious convictions as an individual citizen although he should realize that there is always the tacit representation of one's institution in whatever he says." [26]

The interpretive development of AAUP norms designed to minimize or eliminate any "tacit representation" of the university of course supplements the AATS Statement in this respect: The theologian need not expressly disclaim that he is speaking for his institution so long as he affirms that he is speaking in his individual capacity.[27]

Finally, the AAUP recognition of manifest incompetence and

dereliction of duty as the sole grounds for questioning fitness to teach is given substance in the theological context of the AATS Statement:

> *So long as the teacher remains within the accepted constitutional and confessional basis of his school* he should be free to teach, carry on research, and to publish, subject to his adequate performance of his academic duties as agreed upon with the school." [28]

Clearly the norm of fitness to teach in theology schools is whether the individual operates within the pale of his confessional commitment. A professor whose declarations or actions were beyond the pale of responsible Roman Catholic theological activity could thereby manifest incompetence to teach *Roman Catholic* theology. Under the accepted standards of AATS, declarations or actions within the pale of Roman Catholic theological activity would clearly give no cause to challenge fitness to teach. Moreover, since such declarations or actions would *a fortiori* be "supportable" within the framework of Roman Catholic confessional commitment, they could not be challenged as exceeding the limits of appropriate restraint contemplated by AAUP and, by implication, by AATS.[29] The AATS Statement also clearly subscribes to the basic notion of responsible academic procedure that any challenge respecting fitness to teach (in this instance, challenges that declarations or actions are not within the pale of responsible theological activity according to a particular faith commitment) should be heard and determined by professional peers.[30] The AATS Statement makes clear that *full* academic freedom is perfectly consistent with Christian education, and that any problem arising from Church sponsorship and faith commitment can and should be dealt with through generally applicable modes of academic procedure.

Expert testimony on the norms of AATS was presented to the Inquiry Board by Dr. John Coleman Bennett, President of Union Theological Seminary. President Bennett testified that the spirit of the norms of AATS with respect to extramural expression of the faculty members is the same as the intention of the statement of norms of extramural expression found in the 1940 Statement of AAUP. He said that AATS was not attempting to apply more stringent norms of extramural expression to theologians than the norms of AAUP which are applicable to academicians generally, that the AAUP concept of professional competence is a suitable measure for the fitness to teach of theology professors and that, under AATS formulations, professional competence in the theological context would turn in part on whether the professor theologizes within the pale of his institution's confessional commitment.

Notes

1. 53 *AAUP Bulletin* 369 (Winter 1967).
2. *Ibid.*
3. *Ibid.*
4. *Ibid.*
5. *Id.* at 370–71.
6. Academic Freedom and Tenure: St. Mary's College (Minnesota), 54 *AAUP Bulletin* 37 (Spring 1968).
7. *Id.* at 42 (emphasis supplied).
8. *Ibid.* (emphasis supplied).
9. Academic Freedom and Tenure: Mercy College, 49 *AAUP Bulletin* 245 (Autumn 1963).
10. *Id.* at 247–48.
11. *Id.* at 248.
12. *Id.* at 246 (emphasis supplied).
13. *Id.* at 250 (emphasis supplied).
14. Academic Freedom and Tenure: Gonzaga University, 51 *AAUP Bulletin* 8 (Spring 1965).
15. *Id.* at 15.
16. J. W. Kilgore, "Can Church Related Schools Meet The Present Crisis In Higher Education?" *The Baylor Line* 18–19 (January–February 1966). Professor Kilgore was Chairman of the Special Committee of AAUP on Academic Freedom in Church-related Colleges and Universities.
17. It would be interesting to see a public written rationale of a restriction applicable to the Theologians' Statement.
18. Advisory Letter No. 17, "Questions of Religious Limitation," 51 *AAUP Bulletin* 72 (Spring 1965) (emphasis supplied).

19. American Association of Theological Schools, "Academic Freedom and Tenure in the Theological School," *Bulletin 24* (1960), as reprinted in *Bulletin 27* (1966) at 40 (hereinafter "AATS Statement").
20. *Ibid.*
21. *Ibid.*
22. *Ibid.*
23. 1940 Statement, Paragraph (b); see Report on Church-related Universities, Recommendation 2.
24. AATS Statement 41.
25. 1940 Statement, Paragraph (b).
26. AATS Statement 41.
27. See pp. II–21 to II–26 *supra*.
28. AATS Statement 41 (emphasis supplied).
29. See text cited at note 16 *supra*.
30. See AATS Statement 41.

7

The Inquiry:
The Catholic Confessional
Commitment—Interpretations,
Ambiguities and Enforcement

*"I also embrace and retain each and every thing regarding
the doctrine of faith and morals, whether defined by solemn
judgment or asserted and declared by the ordinary magisterium, as they are proposed by the Church. . . ."—Profession
of Faith, Vatican Congregation for the Teaching of the Faith,
May 31, 1967.*

Despite the doubt expressed by Catholic University Trustees in the
December 23 letter to the Faculty Inquiry Board, standards of
responsible exercise of academic freedom in matters of public
debate and controversy manifestly *are* in existence. These standards are endorsed by American universities and the American
academic community generally; and the American academic
community generally agrees that these standards apply with full
force and equal measure to Church-related colleges and universities. AAUP case studies cited in Chapter Six and other investigations concerning various Roman Catholic institutions of higher
learning indicate that the generally accepted norms of responsible
academic procedure for universities and faculty members have
not necessarily been accepted in practice at all times by the Catholic academic community. Specifically, certain Catholic universi-

99

ties have given evidence that they are not prepared to accept their obligation "as a member of the academic community of higher education in the United States and therefore to share the goals, traditions, ideals, and spirit of that community . . . to withstand and to defend [the university and its faculty] against 'censure' by its 'constituency' when the cause of the criticism is the responsible exercise of academic freedom by members of its faculty." The *Caldwell, Shelton* and *Tench* cases, which together show AAUP's insistence that no Church-related school may enforce special restrictions on extramural expression, also serve to indicate the abuse of administrative or governing board authority in some American Catholic universities, generally in the name of institutional loyalty.

The criteria invoked in the *Caldwell, Shelton* and *Tench* cases show from the beginning the restrictive effects of certain more or less traditional normative provisions commonly found in the statutes and catalogues of Catholic colleges. These norms are of several varieties but all have the same generally restrictive tenor: for example, the rule against "scandal" invoked in the *Caldwell* case, and the rule proscribing "grave offense against Catholic . . . morality" found in the regulations of the college which terminated Professor Tench.

Perhaps the best illustration in Church-related schools of a traditional provision susceptible of an overrestrictive interpretation is the "confessional commitment," referred to in the AATS Statement. In Roman Catholic colleges and universities, this confessional commitment requirement is expressed in the formula of the Profession of Faith. The Profession of Faith was at the center of the *Catholic University* case beginning at least at the September 5 Trustees' meeting. Article 50 of the Catholic University's Vatican Statutes requires all Catholic faculty members to make a Profession of Faith. Cardinal McIntyre in the September 5 Trustees' meeting moved for the "resignation" of the subject professors since their dissent, in his view, had violated their Profession of Faith and thereby terminated their appointments at the University. Since the Profession of Faith is the most extensively used "limitation" in Catholic universities and at the same time a theological proposition in need of interpretation, it is necessary to recall its precise scope and import.

In point of fact, a Catholic Profession of Faith obviously imposes no limitation whatever beyond adherence to and participation in the Roman Catholic Church community. If a person is a Roman Catholic, he has no problem making the Profession; if he is not a Roman Catholic, he is not required to make it. On May 31, 1967, the Vatican Congregation for the Teaching of the Faith issued a new formula to be used when a Profession of Faith is prescribed, in place of the Tridentine formula and the Oath Against Modernism. The new formula reads:

I (name) with firm faith believe and profess each and everything contained in the symbol of faith, namely:

(There follows the Nicene-Constantinopolitan Creed, called the 'Nicene Creed,' familiar from liturgical use. That is followed by this additional statement:)

I also embrace and retain each and every thing regarding the doctrine of faith and morals, whether defined by solemn judgment or asserted and declared by the ordinary magisterium, *as they are proposed by the Church,* especially those things which concern the mystery of the holy Church of Christ, its Sacraments, the Sacrifice of the Mass, and the Primacy of the Roman Pontiff. (Emphasis added.)

This formula, obviously, is composed of two parts. The first part, whose object is the Nicene-Constantinopolitan symbol, is to be believed and professed by firm faith (*firma fide credo et profiteor*). The second part, whose object is an all-inclusive category of teachings, is to be firmly embraced and retained (*firmiter . . . amplector et retineo*), as they are proposed by the Church (*prout ab ipsa proponuntur*). Thus, the second part of the Profession of Faith formula itself implicitly acknowledges the several levels of teaching and diverse binding force of each. The phrase, "as they are proposed by the Church," makes it clear that the Profession of Faith intends a binding force proportionate to the level and quality of each particular teaching. Some teachings are to be believed by *divine faith* since they are proposed by the Church, whether through an infallible definition or by the ordinary universal magisterium, *as divinely revealed*; some teachings are to be held under an absolute binding force since they are *infallibly* proposed, although not of divine faith strictly so-called; other teachings are to be held by that "religious assent" (inherently conditional in nature) which is due to authoritative noninfallible pronouncements.

The sincere and full adherence to the Profession of Faith by no means precludes the right of responsible dissent from authoritative, noninfallible teachings by competent persons under certain qualifications. The confessional commitment, or "faith commitment," attested to by the Profession of Faith required of Catholic faculty members by Catholic University may be preserved intact even in the instance of responsible dissent from noninfallible teachings of the papal or episcopal ordinary magisterium. The relevant question under the Profession is whether, under the circumstances, public dissent from a particular authoritative, noninfallible pronouncement of the papal magisterium is within the pale of supportable Roman Catholic theological options, a question that can be readily posed under the relevant general AAUP norms concerning professional competence in a given academic field: in this instance, Catholic theology. Moreover, and in the same vein, a public expression by a teacher does not "offend against Catholic doctrine" in violation of Article 66 of Catholic University's Statutes so long as it is within the pale of responsible Roman Catholic theological activity, as determined by the experts in that particular academic specialty; *i.e.,* faculty peers.

A distinct problem might to some be posed by the "pontifical" status of a number of Catholic universities throughout the world, including The Catholic University of America. Expert testimony was delivered on the question of pontifical status by Professor John H. Thirlkel, S.S., Dean of the Faculty of Theology, St. Mary's Seminary and University, Baltimore, Maryland, a pontifically chartered faculty.

Dean Thirlkel testified that no inquiry, threat of suspension or other disciplinary proceeding had been instituted by the Trustees of his pontifical institution (whose Statutes are comparable to Catholic University's, including the Profession of Faith) because of the dissent or the style and method of dissent expressed by those faculty members at St. Mary's who subscribed to the Statement by Catholic Theologians. Dean Thirlkel explained that Cardinal Shehan, the Archbishop of Baltimore and Chancellor of St. Mary's, without publicity of any kind, had inquired what the St. Mary's subscribers intended to teach in the classroom and, upon being informed that they would of course teach the Encyclical as "official" teaching of the Church and treat the dissent as a *dissent,* was content to drop the matter.

Dean Thirlkel also testified that the standards of responsibility for faculty members in pontifical universities are not different from the standards applicable at Catholic universities generally. In his opinion as the Dean of a Pontifical theology faculty, the subject professors, in their declarations and actions with respect to the Encyclical, had not violated their obligations under the Pontifical Statutes of the University, specifically including the Profession of Faith. He noted that Pontifical status is purely an academic degree-granting privilege which does not alter the faith commitment of teachers of Roman Catholic theology at such institutions.

Particularly in the context of misunderstanding of "pontifical" status, however, certain Statutes at Catholic University are susceptible of overly restrictive interpretations. For instance, the University is said to "venerate(s) the Roman Pontiff as its Supreme Ruler and Teacher and submit(s) unreservedly to his Apostolic Authority as the only safe norm of truth" (Article 7, English text of the canonical Statutes of the University). Article 66 of the Statutes, in addition to enjoining offenses against Catholic doctrine, provides for a special three-bishop court to adjudicate such "offenses"; moreover, Article 21 enjoins the Chancellor of the University to "safeguard the orthodoxy of doctrine." Such regulations as the foregoing often involve special procedures, such as those in Article 66, which seriously depart from academic due process. Violation of Catholic doctrine could be punished administratively and summarily just as it was at the college involved in the *Tench* case. Catholic University's Article 66 is itself a most blatant offense against academic due process, specifically because by its terms it cedes the power of "final adjudication" to nonpeer "authorities" extrinsic to the University. In addition to these procedural aberrations, however, such rules have an important deterrent effect on free inquiry and expression because of the possibilities of broadly restrictive interpretations. Close theological analysis, however, reveals that restrictive interpretations are not warranted by the terms of these Statutes themselves. Those who would read such norms to call for a kind of para-orthodoxy or superloyalty to the sponsoring Church institution or the incumbents of high Church offices (i.e., those who would interpret "the orthodoxy of doctrine" or "Catholic doctrine" more broadly than the faith commitment) both violate academic freedom and reject the only sensible meaning of the words they interpret.

"Veneration" of the Pope, rightly understood, should not restrict academic freedom. Catholics should understand the idiom well: by virtue of their faith-commitment, they believe that the Pope possesses and exercises a special ruling and teaching office in the Church. He is recognized as "supreme teacher" through the eyes of faith and in terms of the Petrine prerogative regarding the supernatural mystery of salvation, and not in the "academic" sense of the word "teacher," which is the usage in other Articles of the Statutes and in normal academic terminology.

The assertion that the University submits unreservedly to the Pope's Apostolic Authority as the only safe norm of truth is indeed a theological proposition. It is important in this context to recall that the Catholic faith recognizes no real contradiction whatsoever between "natural truth" and "revealed truth," between science and gospel, between faith and reason. "Apparent" contradictions may occasionally appear, but *real* contradictions are a priori considered to be impossible.

The "Apostolic Authority" enjoyed by the Roman Pontiff as "Supreme Teacher" is, therefore, a *doctrinal* authority, not a juridic or jurisdictional authority. Various exercises of the doctrinal authority of the Pope in the Church establish different norms of truth. One such norm of truth is constituted by that exercise of the Apostolic Authority known as an "authoritative, noninfallible" teaching. The norm in this instance would be "safe" in the sense that the truth of the teaching is presumptively certain to Catholics, but that does not exclude the possibility of falsity. Papal exercise of authoritative, noninfallible doctrinal teaching authority is not the "only" example of such teaching; Catholics acknowledge that the ordinary magisterium of bishops (itself an "Apostolic Authority") can also teach in a way which constitutes an authoritative, noninfallible norm. Hence, the term "only" in Catholic University's Statutes should be read to mean "in a special manner proper to the Roman Pontiff as the holder of the Petrine office in the Church." Any other reading would exclude the conciliar magisterium or the ordinary episcopal magisterium as normative of truth.

The Latin text of Catholic University's Statutes makes this interpretive point more clear. The Latin is much more direct and obvious than the English text. The literal translation of the Latin Article 7 states: "The University honors the Roman Pontiff as its supreme Guide and Teacher and adheres with full compliance to His Apostolic authority as a most safe [*tutissimae normae veritatis*] norm of truth." The word "only" in the English text is evidently gratuitously inserted (by comparison with the Latin). The Latin word *"tutissimae"* is simply the superlative adjectival form, which implicitly acknowledges the positive and comparative possibilities of "safe" norms of truth. The Latin superlative adjectival form (unlike English) admits of a simple affirmative sense, *viz.,* "very safe."

Most of the foregoing rules and regulations (except the Article 66 procedures) thus can be interpreted in a manner consistent with both full-fledged "university" and "Catholic" status. However, such rules and regulations, common at other Catholic universities, have at times been interpreted much more restrictively and have been complemented over the years by monitory provisions in official catalogues, bulletins and policy statements which carry forward a decidedly paternalistic theme and complicate the assimilation of Catholic schools into an acceptable academic framework. John L. McKenzie, S.J., Professor of Sacred Scripture at the University of Notre Dame, has pointed out the extra-university source of such restrictive interpretations and provisions and the interventions they invite:

> The fear of disturbing the good faith of the laity is regarded as a sufficient motive for invoking the hierarchy with petitions to arrest those scholarly discussions and opinions which the petitioners judge to be disturbing. Whether it be wise or prudent or not, the hierarchy is likely to think that if many people say they are disturbed, they are disturbed; they may even think that if a few people say many are disturbed, then many are disturbed.[2]

Similarly, in 1963, a Special Faculty Committee Report on Departures from Proper Academic Procedure at Catholic University drew attention to a persistent undue sensitivity to controversy involving Church-related matters:

> *A conspicuous element in the pattern which emerges from the evidence has the appearance of an attempt to make a definite policy of avoidance of intellectual as well as any other kind of controversy in areas which are regarded as sensitive.* This policy has been made explicit in some of the cases which the committee has considered, it is easily imputed in others in which members of the several faculties of the University have been directly or indirectly inhibited or penalized in research or teaching or public expression on subjects within their fields of specialized competence. As has been shown, the means used to implement the policy in question have included censorship of faculty as well as student proposals for lectures, refusal of approval for faculty applications for research funds from foundations, disapproval of academically sound topics of dissertation research, disapproval of proposals for teaching appointments, and even termination of an appointment carrying tenure.
>
> *Matters of scholarship in biblical studies, liturgy, ecclesiology, relations with non-Catholics, evolutionary theory, population problems,*

and sexual behavior are among the subjects which have been treated as controversial. Some of these are indeed subjects of lively controversy at present, others were perhaps once so but can be considered controversial only in a very remote sense today.[3]

Catholic University has been periodically subject to this type of pressure. In the early 1960's, for example, the Faculty Report concluded:

In any case, a policy which seeks to avoid these subjects in research, teaching, or educational discussion because they are in some sense controversial is incompatible with the declared aims of this University or university institutions in general.[4]

This policy of avoidance of intellectual theological controversies further evidenced in the call for the Inquiry and the suspension of dissenters ordered by the University Trustees on September 5, 1968, has had repercussions for Catholic University itself. In the American theological community, Catholic University has had (despite its history of defense of such controversial figures as Professor J. A. Ryan) a reputation of undue harassment of theologians and theological inquiry. In addition, some promising theologians have left Catholic University, in part because of such harassment, according to the testimony of Professor Gerard Sloyan of Temple University, a cleric who formerly served as Head of the Department of Religious Education at Catholic University, Furthermore, theological studies at the University have been woefully underfinanced.[5]

Restrictive interpretations of the duties of the Catholic faith at Catholic University and other Catholic institutions of higher learning seem designed to foster a policy of para-orthodoxy as a safeguard of "the Catholic atmosphere" of the institution. For example:

The institution's "whole life is lived in the Catholic atmosphere, which assumes that earthly life is to be lived * * * in terms of a preparation for the future life with God," and to that end, it "harmonizes" its entire "program with the philosophy and theology of the Catholic Church." The entire program of the College is so ordered "that [the

student's life and study and the atmosphere of the college are per-
meated, motivated, enlarged and integrated by the Catholic way of
life . . ." [College of Notre Dame, Baltimore, Maryland.] [6]

A member of the teaching staff may not teach as true what he knows
to be false, or teach as a fact or as a universal law what is yet but
hypothesis or theory. He may, if he wishes, express his own opinions,
but they must be declared such and not facts. He may not teach anything contradictory to established truth, whether this truth be definitely
known of itself, or from unquestioned human authority, or from the
Catholic Church speaking within its lawful sphere. Obviously within
this scope no one may teach anything injurious to the welfare of the
United States of America. [7]

The latter language found in Catholic University's Faculty Handbook of 1956 was expanded in a statement available in the Office
of the Dean of the College of Arts and Sciences in the late 1950's:

Catholic University differs in the following respects from many
institutions of learning in America:

(a) It proclaims that it does indoctrinate, in the sense that it posi-
tively teaches a system of values and tries to impart to its students
certain definite principles of life and action.

(b) Because it is not only American but Catholic Christian, it
recognizes a somewhat larger number of absolutes than are recognized
by an institution not under Catholic auspices. For instance, it adheres
to the Apostles' Creed as absolute truth and to the teaching of the
Catholic Church as unerring guide in matters of faith and morals. [8]

The first of the foregoing examples was taken from a citation
in a Maryland Supreme Court decision which overturned state
grants for the construction of science classroom buildings to various
colleges, including Notre Dame of Baltimore, on grounds, among
others, that the policy statements of that institution evidenced the
fundamentally sectarian (as distinguished from educational) purposes of the institution, thus implicating the state in a violation of
the First Amendment of the U.S. Constitution as made applicable
to the States by the Fourteenth Amendment by aiding an establishment of religion. [9]

The same basic legal problem recognized by the Maryland Court

could also be lurking in the terms of Article 66 of the Catholic
University Statutes:

If a Teacher offends against Catholic Doctrine or is guilty of grave
misconduct, the matter shall be brought to the Board of Trustees, who
shall submit the whole case to three Bishops for investigation and
final adjudication, with due regard for the rules of the University, in
the case of a cleric, for the regulations of Canon Law.

Action against a teacher under this type of process is of questionable legal validity as well as being a rejection of responsible
academic procedure. Catholic University was incorporated in the
District of Columbia under chapter 18 of the Revised Statutes
of the United States relating to the District of Columbia on April
19, 1887, and the University has since elected to be governed by
the provisions of the District of Columbia Non-Profit Corporation
Act.[10] Approximately two years after its civil incorporation, the
University was designated as a canonical moral person by the Holy
See and given its ecclesiastical Statutes under which it in fact
operates. For example, its President is actually designated by the
Vatican in accordance with Article 23, whereas according to its
civil charter the right and the duty to appoint its President is vested
in its Board of Trustees. However, these Statutes are nowhere
mentioned in the corporate documents on file in the District of
Columbia recording offices. The latest document filed states that
the internal governing rules of the University are its "by-laws," a
distinct document from the Statutes.

A charter of incorporation is in a sense a contract with the civil
authority obligating the institution to fulfill the purposes and terms
of such charter. Even the Code of Canon Law provides for the
canonical acceptance of the governing civil authority's law of contract.[11] Catholic University, therefore, and its Trustees, are obli-
gated to fulfill their duties under the civil law of the District of
Columbia even in respect of the relationship between the University and its ecclesiastical sponsors, including the American hierarchy.

As a general principle of corporation law, reflected in the D.C.

Non-Profit Corporation Act,[12] the business of the corporation should be managed by its Board of Directors: in the case of Catholic University, by its Trustees. Corporate Trustees may delegate the performance of any act which they themselves can perform to officers or agents of the corporation (or even, in some jurisdictions, to strangers to the corporation) so long as such delegation is a reasonable, honest exercise of judgment. Some jurisdictions, however, somewhat limit the power of corporate directors of Trustees to delegate discretionary powers. It is nevertheless clear that such Directors or Trustees may not agree to exercise their official responsibilities for the benefit of anyone other than the corporation or for any "good" purpose other than the corporation's purposes.[13]

A recent study of the civil and canonical status of Catholic institutions in the United States undertaken by the Reverend John McGrath, now President of St. Mary's College of South Bend, Indiana, has emphasized the distinction between Catholic educational and charitable institutions as corporate entities and the Church institutions which sponsor them.[14] The McGrath study demonstrates that the legal character of a corporation is determined solely from its charter, not from the intent of its sponsors. Thus, the question for Catholic University is whether its Trustees may manage the affairs of the University in keeping with the best interest of the sponsors of the University—the American hierarchy—when those interests conflict with the best interests of the corporation as an educational entity of university rank. The McGrath study underscored one of the more significant early cases in this field, a decision which determined the constitutionality of a federal aid grant to a Catholic-sponsored hospital—*Bradfield v. Roberts*.[15] The Commissioners of the District of Columbia had paid to Providence Hospital—whose business was conducted by the Daughters of Charity—certain sums (calculated on the basis of the number of poor patients served) from funds appropriated by Congress. The Court held that neither the appropriation nor the payments violated the First Amendment of the Constitution; the

Court based its decision on the corporate character of the institution, ruling that whether the individuals who compose the corporation under its charter happen to be all Roman Catholics or members of any other religious sect "is of not the slightest consequence with reference to the law of its incorporation:"

Nor is it material that the hospital may be conducted under the auspices of the Roman Catholic Church . . . . That fact does not alter the legal character of the corporation, which is incorporated under an act of Congress, and its powers, duties and character are to be solely measured by the charter under which it alone has any legal existence.[16]

In respect of Providence Hospital, the Court subscribed to the lower court's reasoning:

This corporation "is not declared the trustee of any church or religious society. Its property is to be acquired in its own name and for its own purposes; that property and its business are to be managed in its own way, *subject to no visitation, supervision or control by any ecclesiastical authority whatever* but only to that of the Government which created it." [17]

The distinction between the corporate institution and its sponsoring body set forth in the *Bradfield* case provides a salient norm for the management of Church-sponsored universities. It suggests that charitable and educational institutions conducted under the auspices of the American Catholic hierarchy, for example, will be recognized as secular corporate institutions but only so long as it is not evident that the institution is operatively subject to its distinct sponsoring body. Under Canon Law, moreover, the Trustees of Catholic University owe a prior duty to their civil corporate obligations.[18] Consequently, in cases in which the good of Catholic University as an educational civil corporation conflicts with the desires of its sponsoring body or individual financial sponsors, the stated civil purposes of the University must prevail.

Notes

1. *Acta Apostolicae Sedis,* Vol. LIX, p. 1058 (emphasis supplied).
2. J. McKenzie, S.J., "Faith and Intellectual Freedom," *The Critic,* Vol. XX, No. 1, 8, 69 (August-September 1961).
3. "Report of A Special Committee on Departure From Proper Academic Procedure," commissioned by Faculty of Graduate School of Arts and Sciences, The Catholic University of America, 12 (1963) (emphasis supplied).
4. *Ibid.*
5. Heald, Hobson and Associates, Incorporated, "Future Prospects for The Catholic University of America," Report to the Survey and Objectives Committee of the Board of Trustees 22 (1968).
6. See *Horace Mann League v. Bd. of Public Works,* 220 A.2d 51, 70 (Md. Ct. App. 1966), citing stated purposes of College of Notre Dame of Maryland.
7. The Catholic University of America, *Information for the Faculty* 22 (1956) (hereinafter "1956 Handbook").
8. The Catholic University of America "Freedom of Teaching and Research" (apparently an appendix to the 1956 Handbook) (circa 1956).
9. 220 A.2d 51.
10. 29 D.C. Code §§ 1001 *et seq.* (1964).
11. Canon 1529.
12. 29 D.C. Code § 1018 (1964).
13. See generally 19 *Am. Jur.* 2d. §§ 1147, 1162.
14. J. McGrath, *Catholic Institutions in the United States: Canonical and Civil Law Status* (1968).
15. 175 U.S. 291 (1899).
16. *Id.* at 298.
17. *Id.* at 299.
18. Canon 1529; see text at note 10, *supra.*

8

The Inquiry:
Newer Dimensions
of Academic Freedom
in Catholic Universities

*"To perform its teaching and research functions effectively
the Catholic University must have a true autonomy and academic freedom in the face of authority of any kind, lay or
clerical . . ."—Statement on the Nature of the Contemporary
Catholic University, Land O'Lakes, Wisconsin (1967), published under the auspices of the North American Region of
the International Federation of Catholic Universities.*

Leaders of the American Catholic academic community have
taken steps to reconcile the specific purpose of the Catholic universities with the generally accepted notions of responsible academic procedure. One of the editors of a recent symposium at
Notre Dame University on academic freedom in the Catholic university commented that "the new ecumenical spirit of the Church
provides additional and immediate support for the growth of academic freedom in Catholic institutions of higher learning."[1]

The operative concepts of academic freedom, as set forth in the
1940 and 1958 Statements of AAUP, are clearly not inimical
to the Catholic faith commitment and traditional Catholic values.

In a classical idiom, the First Vatican Council (1869-1870)
solemnly taught the impossibility of opposition between faith
and reason, the mutual assistance of faith and reason and the due
freedom of scientific endeavor.

Although faith is above reason, nevertheless, between faith and reason no true dissension can ever exist, since the same God who reveals mysteries and infuses faith has bestowed on the human soul the light of reason; moreover, God cannot contradict himself, nor ever contradict truth with truth. . . .

And, not only can faith and reason never be at variance with one another, but they also bring mutual help to each other. . . . Wherefore, the Church is so far from objecting to the culture of the human arts and sciences, that it aids and promotes this cultivation in many ways.[2]

More recently, the Vatican Council II's *Declaration on Religious Freedom* observed:

The sense of the dignity of the human person has been impressing itself more and more deeply on the consciousness of contemporary man. And the demand is increasingly made that men should act on their own judgment, enjoying and making use of a responsible freedom, not driven by coercion but motivated by a sense of duty.[3]

In *The Pastoral Constitution on the Church in the Modern World,* this teaching was specified in respect to academic freedom:

In order that they may fulfill their functions, let it be recognized that all the faithful, whether clerics or laity, possess a lawful freedom of inquiry, freedom of thought and of expressing their mind with humility and fortitude in those matters on which they enjoy competence.[4]

In the *Declaration on Christian Education,* Vatican II insisted that "individual branches of knowledge [be] studied according to their own proper principles and methods with due freedom of scientific investigation."[5]

In a questionnaire directed to Catholic universities, the Congregation for Catholic Education has affirmed that:

. . . In the spirit of the Second Vatican Council, it can be stated that the Catholic university should be before all else:

a) a community of both teachers and students in search for truth in the context of an integral Christian vision;

b) a center for the development and diffusion of higher culture of an authentic nature for the service of society;

c) a living organism to contribute, in an effective way, along with those who give it life, to the search for solutions to those problems which at this time especially concern mankind.[6]

Since Vatican II particularly, Catholic educators have begun to see true academic freedom as a *necessary* characteristic of a distinctively Catholic university. The President's *Introduction* to the *Faculty Manual of Notre Dame University* confirms the relevance of the Vatican II statements concerning freedom of inquiry to the accepted purposes of a Catholic university:

. . . The University, as *Catholic,* is universal in a double sense; first, its concern touches the moral as well as the intellectual dimensions of all the questions it asks itself and its students, and, secondly, it must emphasize the rightful centrality of Philosophy and Theology among its intellectual concerns if there is to be real adequacy of knowledge in the university, universality in the mind's quest for knowledge and meaning, rightness and relevance, understanding and wisdom.

This dual commitment is more personal than institutional, and can only be made by persons in that atmosphere of freedom which above all must characterize the Catholic university of our day. . . .

There is a vision of all this in Vatican II's Constitution on the Church in the Modern World. . . . This document . . . is the real base for a new character for Catholic universities . . .[7]

The emphasis of the *Notre Dame Faculty Handbook* is reflected in principle by the considered statements of other Catholic institutions and educators throughout the country. The Report of the Ad Hoc Committee for the Study of the Guidelines of Academic Freedom formulated at Dayton University, presented to the faculty of Dayton as a "working paper" for a university statement of objectives, took the following position (as a foundation for its discussion of the relationship between the working theologian and the magisterium):

If anyone is to discuss the purposes of a Catholic university intelligently, then the very first issue which must be settled is the relationship of the university and the Church. Although this relationship is rather complex, we attempt a *description* under two points: 1) the true autonomy of the university; 2) the compatibility of autonomy and a real institutional commitment to the Church.

First of all then, the autonomy of the university. This is the condition *sine qua non* for the existence and survival of the university.

To think of the Catholic university as an instrument of the Church for carrying out its teaching mission leads both to serious misunderstandings of the Church's teaching mission in itself and unfortunately to profound distortions of the nature of the university.[8]

The Dayton Report suggests a possible reconciliation of the respect which a Catholic university shows to the ordinary teaching authority in the Church and the fundamental autonomy which the university asserts in defense of the working principles of academic freedom and responsible academic procedure:

Respect for the official Catholic position does not preclude the possibility of what some scholars have called "loyal opposition." For example, it should not be considered disrespectful to the Church for a professor, Catholic or not, to present the Church's official position and the opposing points of view and then to indicate the reasons why, in his considered judgment, a revision of the Church's position would be in order. This procedure, far from being disrespectful, would really be a service of the academic community to the Magisterium. Such a manner of acting not only shows reverence for the Magisterium but also makes a contribution to the dialog which must take place between the Church and the modern world.[9]

The developing consensus accepted among leaders in the Catholic academic community emphasizes that the Catholic university must be a university in the authentic contemporary sense of that word; that the generally recognized concept of academic freedom fosters rather than hinders the overall objectives of a Catholic university; and that, specifically, the Catholic university, giving reflective recognition to the accepted principles of academic freedom, should serve as the critical objective intelligence of the Church-society. A culmination of this emerging consensus was the recent promulgation by leading Catholic educators of the Western hemisphere of a "Statement on the Nature of the Contemporary Catholic University." This Statement, generally known as the Land O'Lakes Statement, was published under the auspices of the North American Region of the International Federation of Catholic Universities. The Land O'Lakes Statement asserted in pertinent part:

The Catholic university today must be a university in the full modern sense of the word, with a strong commitment to and concern for academic excellence. *To perform its teaching and research functions effectively the Catholic university must have a true autonomy and academic freedom in the face of authority of whatever kind, lay or clerical, external to the academic community itself.* To say this is simply to assert that institutional autonomy and academic freedom are essential conditions of life and growth and indeed of survival for Catholic universities as for all universities.

. . . Distinctively, then, the Catholic university must be an institution, a community of learners or a community of scholars, in which Catholicism is perceptibly present and effectively operative.

In the Catholic university this operative presence is effectively achieved first of all by the presence of a group of scholars in all branches of theology. . . . Since the pursuit of the theological sciences is therefore a high priority for a Catholic university, *academic excellence in these disciplines becomes a double obligation in a Catholic university.*

Every university, Catholic or not, serves as the critical reflective intelligence of its society. In keeping with this general function, the Catholic university has the added obligation of performing this same service for the Church. Hence, the university should carry on a continual examination of all aspects and all activities of the Church and should objectively evaluate them. The Church would thus have the benefit of continual counsel from Catholic universities. Catholic universities in the recent past have hardly played this role at all. It may well be one of the most important functions of the Catholic university of the future.[10]

The 1968 Statement of the International Federation of Catholic Universities reflected the expression in the Land O'Lakes Statement that the presence of theology, with the full enjoyment of academic freedom, was the ideal and normal operative Catholic

presence in the Catholic university[11] The Federation Statement
described a series of activities proper to a Catholic university, including the following:

> To make theology relevant to all human knowledge and all human
> knowledge relevant to theology itself;
> To put at the disposal of the people of God and especially of those
> with responsibility for making serious decisions in the church the dis-
> coveries of knowledge in every field.[12]

The Federation Statement further noted that "to these special
tasks Catholic universities are dedicated by an institutional commitment which includes a respect for and a voluntary acceptance
of the Church's teaching authority."[13]

The Federation Statement leaves open the question whether the
"respect" and "voluntary acceptance" of the Church's teaching authority in any way infringes on the commitment to be a university
in the full modern sense of the word. However, the Land O'Lakes
Statement emphasized what is apparently a developing consensus
on this question in asserting the functional autonomy necessary
in any Catholic university and the compatibility of full academic
freedom with religious goals.

However, some Catholic academicians stand opposed to accepting the principles of academic freedom. For example, the editor
of the Notre Dame symposium on academic freedom contrasts the
generally accepted principles of academic freedom "with a second,
modified view of academic freedom which has been advanced as
necessary for the maintenance of the identity of a truly Catholic
university."[14]

> (1) Over and above the requirements of competence and profes-
> sional ethics, the freedom of the teacher or research worker is limited
> by a specific doctrinal test, of a religious nature. (2) Teaching must
> include among its controls the consideration that a student's "loss of
> faith," or denial of the context of the doctrinal test, reflects unfavor-
> ably upon the quality and integrity of the pedagogical process. (3) In
> contested cases, it is permissible to invoke administrative or ecclesias-
> tical authority—from which there is no appeal—in order to maintain
> doctrinal purity.[15]

The symposium editor, of course, concluded that such *modified* "freedom" was inconsistent with accepted concepts of academic liberty:

> . . . It is one thing to hold that churches are free to support or control institutions of higher learning, or even that the common good of a free, pluralistic society may require them to do so, and another thing to identify the institutions so controlled as truly free universities, or as universities whose faculties enjoy full academic freedom.[16]

However, dissent within the American Catholic educational community with respect to the full acceptance of the principles of university autonomy and academic freedom as set forth in the Land O'Lakes Statement has persisted. Professor Germain Grisez, for example, of Georgetown University, disagrees in principle with the Land O'Lakes Statement:

> . . . The Statement asserts: "To perform its teaching and research functions effectively the Catholic university must have a true autonomy and academic freedom in the face of authority of any kind, lay or clerical, external to the academic community itself." The committee goes on to state that the presence of a theological faculty, interdisciplinary communication, and an effort to live in the Christian spirit should distinguish a Catholic university. Not a word is said about faith and its proper and primary role in Christian intellectual life. Specifics concerning the principles of theology and the Catholic mode of life have been so carefully avoided that the characterization, intended to be of the Catholic university, probably is better fulfilled by Yale or the University of Chicago than by any of the institutions whose administrators signed the document.[17]

Professor Grisez defends the application of financial pressure particularly to enforce views of a Catholic's academic responsibility which would deny legitimate Roman Catholic theological options.[18]

The issue between the point of view represented by Professor Grisez and the point of view represented by the Land O'Lakes Statement is most sharply focused in the "sacred sciences," the most Church-related of all academic disciplines. The special relationship of Catholic theologians (and other sacred science scholars) to the Church calls for great care in evaluating public "extramural" expressions by theologians. Such expressions, because of the Church sponsorship of the school, might be expected to have intramural effects; but such effects must be carefully distinguished from indications of unfitness to teach, a matter to be judged solely in terms of professional competence.

A recent statement on the rights and freedoms basic to the Christian community, "Towards a Declaration of Christian Freedoms," promulgated by the Canon Law Society of America, emphasized the compatibility and indeed the harmony between the Roman Catholic faith-commitment and the full scope of intellectual freedom, particularly as exercised by scholars of the sacred sciences:

> Within the tradition exemplified by *Pacem in Terris, Mater et Magistra, Gaudium et Spes* (The Pastoral Constitution of the Church in the Modern World, the Second Vatican Council), the United Nations Universal Declaration of Human Rights and the United States Bill of Rights, we affirm the following inalienable and inviolable rights and freedoms of persons in the Christian community:
>
> The right to freedom in the search for truth, without fear of administrative sanctions. We affirm in particular the right to develop conceptual and metaphysical systems aimed at reflecting the dynamic character of the universe and of human society within it. The Church neither stands nor falls on any system of "perennial philosophy" or an established metaphysics.
>
> The right to freedom in expressing personal beliefs and opinions as they appear to the individual, including freedom of communication and publication. *In particular, we affirm the right of competent persons to express dissent from doctrines that are taught authoritatively but not infallibly.* We wish to emphasize the special significance of these rights for persons working in the scholarly community, where freedom of discovery and expression are the clearest safeguards of truth.[19]

Other professional discussions of the role of theological scholarship in Catholic universities have emphasized the rightful claim of theologians to the full benefits of principles of academic freedom, particularly in respect of the role of the magisterium.

In the matter of doctrine the problem is best examined by contrasting the task of the theologian and the charism of the bishop. The task of the theologian is to reflect on the Word of God and to explore its dimension in every direction. The task of the bishop is to be an official witness of the presence and the identity of the Word of God in the Church. The task of the theologian and the charism of the bishop are not identical; they are rather complementary. The Church needs them both. However, before the ideal state of harmony is reached many difficulties may arise.

The theologian is the explorer of the Word of God. In his endeavor he has to use scientific methods of construing hypotheses and trying to verify them through the available data of revelation. In doing so he is exploring unknown fields. He is attempting to bring clarity where there was previously obscurity, understanding where there was ignorance. In this research he is subject to mistakes. Through mistakes he advances towards corrections and better solutions.

In theological research and teaching, condemnations would be out of place at a modern university. Yet, in an extreme case the bishops would be fully entitled to state that a given teaching does not express the belief of the Catholic community. This should be done without condemning the person concerned. It should be done as a matter of clarification.[20]

One of the participants in the Open Session of the 1968 Easter Meeting of the Jesuit Education Association posed the key question for Catholic university theology:

What if the Pope and all the bishops decided that Professor X was not teaching Catholic dogma? The scholar himself should examine their pronouncement, should ask about the obligations he has as a Catholic, but he should not be removed because of the ecclesiastical decision. The scholar might be removed but his own peers should make the judgment.[21]

Of course, the question of heresy was not truly involved in the Inquiry into dissent at Catholic University; rather, the questions framed by the Trustees reflected the imposition of one possible theological option to the exclusion of another. (Some had questioned whether the dissenters had violated their Profession of Faith, but, as noted herein, a proper theological interpretation of that profession shows that there is not a scintilla of support for such questions.)

Those Catholic educators who have accepted a full commitment to responsible academic procedure and academic freedom have accepted the standard of *faith* and not of para-orthodoxy as the maximum professional requirement permitted by responsible academic procedure. At the same time, they have relied precisely on the unfettered presence of the academic discipline of theology as the surest means of maintaining Catholicity on the campus. The commitment made in the Land O'Lakes Statement to regard theology as a "legitimate intellectual discipline" was made in the context of full acceptance of the principles of academic freedom, particularly in respect of the obligation of universities to guard the freedom of all scholars at the institution from any extrinsic interference. Even prescinding from the university context, it is not in the interest of good theologizing in and for the Church that theologians be restricted in any measure beyond the boundaries of their faith commitment. If, in terms of this faith commitment, the declarations or actions of a theologian prove to be, to the satisfaction of his peers, "within the pale of responsible Roman Catholic theological activity" and within the norms of expression set forth by AAUP, he should be protected in his work by the generally accepted principles of academic freedom affirmed by the American academic and theological community (particularly in the AATS Statement). And he should not be subject to extrinsic interference of any kind. A scholarly community where such a theologian is resident owes a duty under these accepted principles of academic freedom and responsible academic procedure to protect him from "authority of whatever kind, lay or clerical, external to the academic community itself."

President Theodore M. Hesburgh, in addition to his particular testimony concerning the subject professors' compliance with the AAUP norms, addressed additional written testimony to the Inquiry Board setting forth his support for the full application of the principles of academic freedom in Church-related schools. He informed the Board that his own position was best indicated by the Land O'Lakes Statement, and by the University of Notre Dame Faculty Handbook, which specifically adopts the 1940 Statement of norms of faculty extramural expression set forth by AAUP.

President Victor Yanitelli of St. Peter's College testified that the standards of academic responsibility generally accepted in American universities were perfectly adequate as norms for faculty expression in Church-related colleges and universities. President Yanitelli thus supplemented the testimony of President Cross of Hunter College (now of Swarthmore College) to the effect that any question of "orthodoxy" could be handled as a question of professional competence in teaching areas where "orthodoxy" might be relevant, such as "Roman Catholic" theology. President Yanitelli also made clear that, from his point of view "the allegiance of the theologian can, . . . if it is understood in the context of the American University and the context of the American Church, be a total allegiance. But he has got to have the freedom to pursue his specialty." Further, he affirmed that a Catholic university should resist arbitrary exercises of ecclesiastical power such as the unwarranted transfers of "dissenters" or "controversial" professors who happened to be priests back to some quiet nonacademic duties.

Expert testimony on the question of norms applicable in Catholic universities was also delivered by The Reverend Doctor Clarence W. Friedman, Associate Secretary, College and University Department, National Catholic Education Association. Doctor Friedman testified that the matter of academic freedom and due process is the most vital issue facing Catholic higher education now and in the future, even more important than the problem of attaining adequate financial support: "A university can afford to be poor but not unfree." Like President Yanitelli, Doctor Friedman not only affirmed that the professors had done no wrong under the accepted norms of academic responsibility applicable in all universities, including Catholic schools of theology, but also went beyond the necessities of the case and suggested means whereby university Trustees could avoid making mistakes in the sensitive area of academic freedom. He prefaced his observations by recognizing a specific problem faced by The Catholic University of America, caused by the unspoken and unwarranted assumption that the American Catholic hierarchy has such an intrinsic relationship with the University that the University Trustees must either endorse or negate each publicly uttered view on a controversial theological subject made by University faculty members. Of course, competent advice on academic freedom and responsible academic procedure would disabuse the University Trustees of that view; Doctor Friedman pointed out that "In this highly technical and professional sort of thing . . . it is very difficult for the nonprofessional or the amateur to deal with these highly complex problems of higher education." He testified that Trustees, in his opinion, must not act on academic matters without first obtaining competent advice on the applicable normative considerations. Further, he not only thought that the dissenting professors had acted in complete accord with the generally accepted academic norms but also that the dissent of the theologians "set a model which all universities might imitate in this sense that it was orderly, it was rational; there was no interference with the rights of anyone."

Not all Catholic academicians, however, would accept the foregoing views, particularly with respect to theologians. Professor Grisez writes:

. . . . Some have suggested that theology should be carried on in Catholic colleges and universities on the same basis as all other disciplines, with no special subordination to ecclesiastical authority. But the *magisterium* is related to theology in a special way. Theology must respond to the *magisterium* of the Church much as a natural science must respond to the facts of nature, or better, to the instruments which record these facts. Theologies are falsified when anathematized, just as scientific theories are falsified when the results of experiment go against them. . . .[22]

Accepted Catholic principles of academic responsibility, however, stand against Professor Grisez's view. The Land O'Lakes Statement clearly indicates that leading Catholic educators agree that the accepted standards of academic freedom and responsible academic procedure can and should apply undiluted to all scholarship in Catholic universities, including theology; and that there indeed is no true conflict between adherence to the Roman Catholic faith-commitment and the demands of free scholarly inquiry, both speculative and practical.

The issue is clear for American Catholic universities: should they wholeheartedly subscribe to the fundamental tenets of accepted responsible academic procedure articulated by AAUP and AATS and re-emphasized in the Catholic context by the Land O'Lakes Statement, which asserted the autonomy of intellectual pursuits at Catholic institutions, even in respect of ecclesiastical constituencies of such institutions? The Board of Trustees of Saint Peter's College, as President Yanitelli testified before the Inquiry Board, has given a clear answer in an exemplary statement, endorsing the 1940 Statement of AAUP but excepting the sentence which reads: "Limitations of academic freedom because of religious or other aims of the institution should be clearly stated in writing at the time of the appointment." Saint Peter's President Yanitelli, in announcing the Trustees' decision, declared that the Trustees "also welcome the opportunity to declare that religious belief and religious principles do not, and must never, be used as inhibitors of freedom to pursue the truth wherever that pursuit may lead."[23]

St. Peter's endorsed full academic freedom while Catholic University's Trustees were questioning partial tolerance of extramural freedom. Father Yanitelli, informing the Inquiry Board of his institution's acceptance of the 1940 Statement of AAUP without the "special limitation clause" observed that his Board had specifically "rejected the implication that there was a contradiction between a commitment in faith and academic freedom. We feel that the challenge today is to show that there is not." He explained that he had resisted external pressures "to do something" about the public dissent from the Encyclical at his University: "I saw my function . . . as being the man who promotes and protects debate on debatable questions." He further observed that Catholic educational institutions are "facing the challenge of either going all the way as an American university or becoming a doctrinal institution for catechetical or proselytizing purposes. I don't think the choice is open anymore as to what we must do if we insist or say that we are an American college or . . . university."

President Yanitelli's testimony thus went beyond the necessities of the facts of the case. He dealt with the further question of the overall disciplinary norms applicable in a Church-related university not only to public expressions of dissent but to classroom conduct and teaching as well. He observed that "academic freedom is of a wholeness; you can't have just a little bit of it." Consequently, he felt that not only were restraints on academic freedom unacceptable both in the public arena and in the classroom discussion, but also that such restraints were as inapplicable in the discipline of theology as in any other discipline. He added that questions of "orthodoxy" (as distinguished from para-orthodoxy) could be treated, in the field of "Roman Catholic theology" as questions of professional competence, to be passed on by academic peers, the position taken by the subject professors and President Cross, in their respective written and oral testimony. For example, if a teacher of "Roman Catholic theology" averred publicly that he would teach that Jesus Christ was not God, there would be reason to question his fitness to teach Roman Catholic theology. President Yanitelli explained that any questions of orthodoxy would first be referred to his theology department for professional advice.

Even the Trustees of Catholic University, shortly before convening the Inquiry into dissent, had expressed a forthright assertion of the compatibility of full academic freedom and Christian education. Their Statement of Objectives of July 27, 1968, asserts in no uncertain terms that the University must function as "a free and autonomous center of study" and that its scholars must function in an atomosphere of academic competence where freedom is fostered and where "the only constraint upon truth is truth itself." The Catholic University Trustees said that they accepted "the standards and procedures of American institutions" and called for "proper intellectual and academic witness to Christian faith and humanism."

The action of St. Peter's College is a concrete example of the compatibility of the established American norms of academic freedom with the core principles of Catholic education. There should be no hesitance on the part of any Catholic university to accept the general norms set forth by AAUP and the more specific norms of AATS in respect of theological studies. The AATS norms are, of course, fully consistent with the AAUP standard of academic rights and responsibilities. The principles of academic freedom in theology enunciated by AATS are clearly in harmony with the Land O'Lakes Statement of general Catholic norms *and* the commitment to the search for truth of The Catholic University of America. The controlling principle of AATS is that:

The theological teacher and his students have the inquiry for truth central to their vocation and they are free to pursue this inquiry.

In the context of such strong affirmation of academic freedom, AAUP's continued toleration of "special limitations" in Church-related classrooms is in itself controversial. The question has been asked (perhaps as a result of AAUP's strong defense of extramural freedom in Church-school cases) if *any* toleration by the American academic community of "special limitations" on academic freedom in an area of intellectual pursuit is not a fatal flaw in a set of values in which the pursuit of truth—wherever it leads—is supposed to be paramount. Special limits on classroom freedom are not required to enable Church-related schools to articulate courses in "Roman Catholic theology" or "Lutheran theology" (any more than a university needs a special dispensation to create a course program in "Black studies"). Elimination of the "special limitation" clause of AAUP would in no way infringe the rights of Church-related schools to establish programs of education consonant with their own value orientations. However, it would require Church-related schools to deal with their faculties in terms of peer-established criteria of professional competence in the particular subject matter, not in terms of standards of institutional loyalty having their source outside the academic community.

Notes

1. E. Manier, "Introduction," *The Crisis in American Catholic Higher Education, Academic Freedom and the Catholic University* 3 (E. Manier and J. Houck, eds., 1967) (hereinafter "Manier").
2. H. Denzinger, A. Schoenmetzer, eds., *Enchiridion Symbolorum* ¶¶ 3017, 3019 (32nd ed. 1963).
3. *Declaration on Religious Freedom,* para. 1.
4. *Pastoral Constitution on the Church in the Modern World,* para. 62.
5. *Declaration on Christian Education,* para. 10.
6. See Interdepartmental Communication, The Catholic University of America, Rector Scheel to Members of the Academic Senate, at 2 (February 5, 1969).
7. Introduction, *University of Notre Dame Faculty Manual,* at III, V (1967).
8. Report of the Ad Hoc Committee For the Study of the Guidelines of Academic Freedom, Dayton University (1967), 18, 20, 21.
9. *Id.* at 21.
10. (July 23, 1967) (emphasis supplied).
11. International Federation of Catholic Universities "The Catholic University in the Modern World, (Eighth Triennial Congress, Lovanium University, Kinshasa, Democratic Republic of Congo, 1968), reprinted in *The Catholic University of America, Administrative Bulletin,* Vol. I, No. 5 at 1–3 (October 8, 1968).
12. *Id.* at 2.
13. *Ibid.*
14. Manier 15.
15. *Id.* at 19.
16. *Id.* at 20.
17. G. Grisez, "Academic Freedom and Catholic Faith," *NCEA Bulletin* 15, 17 (November 1967).
18. *Id.* at 18–19.
19. N.C. News Service (Domestic), Oct. 17, 1968.
20. L. Orsy, S.J., "Statement on Academic Freedom at a University" (Paper), at 3.
21. E. Bianchi, S.J., Summary of the J.E.A. Open Session, at 7.
22. G. Grisez, *supra* note 106, at 18.
23. Press Release, St. Peter's College (October 22, 1968).

9

The Inquiry:
Professional Responsibility
in Catholic Theological Dissent

"I agree that the [Statement by Catholic Theologians] can be defended on principles that are acceptable in Catholic theology. . . ."—Letter dated March 6, 1969, of Bernard J. F Lonergan, Research Professor of Systematic Theology, St. Regis College, Toronto, to counsel for the subject professors, for presentation to the Faculty Inquiry Board.

"I think that a method that involves going to the press and television, . . . if the issue is sufficiently important . . . is almost unavoidable . . ."—Testimony of Professor Austin Vaughan, delivered before the Faculty Board of Inquiry.

The materials in the preceding five Chapters show that the rationale of academic freedom, the status of theology as a "sacred science" and the consensus of the university and Catholic intellectual worlds affirm that there is no reason to question the fitness of particular teachers of "Roman Catholic theology" or sacred science to teach, absent:

1) grave violation of the norms of extramural expression in Paragraph (c) of the 1940 Statement of AAUP which gives evidence of professional incompetence;

2) "dereliction of duty," as shown by a material violation of a legitimately prescribed University obligation; or

3) professional incompetence, as evidenced by expressions or

129

modes of expression which are proved to be beyond the pale of the confessional commitment of the university—in this instance, beyond the pale of responsible Roman Catholic theological activity.

Grounds (1) and (2) have been examined in connection with the treatment of the AAUP norms and the university regulations set forth in the previous chapters. The third ground merits special focus, because it perhaps is a novel suggestion in many Catholic circles that questions turning on the "pale" of the Roman Catholic faith-commitment can be formulated and decided by professional peers as questions of professional competence, thus both preserving the autonomy of the academic community and protecting the legitimate interests of the sponsoring church. Peer judgments formulated in the context of professional criteria have the important advantage, additionally, of offering a more reliable guard against imposition of "para-orthodox" restraints in the name of religious loyalty.

Declarations and actions of "Roman Catholic theologians" which indicate that such professors will teach *as* "Roman Catholic theology" that which is not "Roman Catholic theology" are the forms of conduct which trigger inquiry into Roman Catholic theological professional competence. Such actions or declarations, purporting to be "Roman Catholic theology" but not in fact within the pale of responsible Roman Catholic theological activity, could give rise to questions cognizable under AAUP and AATS norms, as to *fitness to teach* that particular academic specialty.

To fulfill their task properly, faculty peers judging the competence of expressions of theologians will find it necessary to make a *functional,* as distinguished from an *ultimate,* theological judgment concerning the declarations and actions of subject professors. If their theological expression is demonstrably heretical or in some other way a violation of their Profession of Faith as Roman Catholics, the question of violation of responsibility would turn in one direction; if their position is a supportable Roman Catholic position, the question of discharge of responsibility necessarily turns in another direction. A *functional* theological judgment does not purport to determine the ultimate truth or falsity of a particular theological position—that lies beyond the scope of the faculty peers such as the Catholic University Board of Inquiry. In cases involving the academic responsibility of sacred science teachers, however, peers can and must ascertain, by an academic evaluation of existing expert judgments, whether a plurality of supportable Catholic positions exists and whether the position taken is within that pale. A panel of peers could not fulfill its function without making a determination as to whether a particular theological declaration or action is within the pale of responsible Roman Catholic theological options. This determination would be intended only, and would operate only, to establish the permissibility or tenability of the particular theological declaration or action without prejudice to the possibility that there may be other, even contradictory, views likewise permissible or tenable. Such a determination is solely for the purpose of determining the university status of the faculty member in question, and does not purport to be an ultimate doctrinal judgment.

When Bishop Shannon, the Trustees' representative, appeared before the Inquiry Board, he was informed that, in view of the Trustees' September 5 mandate for an Inquiry into the dissenting "declarations" and "actions," the Inquiry Board had concluded that it would have to make such a functional theological judgment—that is, that it would have to pass on the theological *tenability* of the dissent, in terms of Roman Catholic theology. Bishop Shannon stated that this was a "reasonable" way for the Inquiry Board to proceed.

This chapter summarizes the expert testimony presented to the Inquiry Board concerning the criteria, more fully set forth in the companion volume, which should be applied to determine whether particular theological activity on the part of Roman Catholic theologians in a university is "responsible," with specific exemplification in terms of the Catholic University controversy. (Those criteria and the other theological materials pertinent to the Theologians' Statement of dissent are fully set forth in the companion volume.)

1) The Question of Dissent. It is within the pale of responsible Roman Catholic theological activity that Roman Catholic theologians may and in some cases even should dissent from authoritative, noninfallible teaching of the hierarchical magisterium when there are sufficient reasons for so doing. The reasons for this assertion are: the interpretive function of the theologian vis-à-vis the tradition in the Church; the co-responsibility of the theologian in and for the Church; the very nature of noninfallible teaching itself; the "common teaching" among the manualists that dissent from authoritative, noninfallible teaching of the papal and hierarchical magisterium is possible; Vatican II's *Constitution on the Church* (*Lumen Gentium*) as interpreted in the light of the *modi* to the document and its historical development; statements of national hierarchies, including the American bishops, which acknowledge the right to dissent from authoritative noninfallible teaching of the hierarchical magisterium; unanimous expert testimony (including that of Professor Peter in the Chancellor's meeting on August 20) that the right to dissent from noninfallible papal teaching is a "common teaching" among Catholic theologians.

Expert testimony of distinguished Catholic theologians, such as Professor Bernard Lonergan, S. J., Research Professor of Systematic Theology at Regis College, Toronto, and member of the Vatican's recently appointed Commission of Theologians, and Professor Walter Burghardt, S.J., Professor of Patristic Theology at Woodstock (Maryland) College, Editor of *Theological Studies* and also a member of the recently appointed Commission of Theologians, confirms the Roman Catholic viability of such dissent. Professor Lonergan succinctly attested to the dissenting professors' written testimony and affirmed that the dissent upheld was supportable "on principles that are acceptable in Catholic theology." Professor Burghardt affirmed explicitly that "it is legitimate under certain circumstances for competent individuals to dissent" from noninfallible pronouncements. Another witness, Professor Austin Vaughan of St. Joseph's Seminary in Yonkers, New York, contended that dissent in the case of *Humanae Vitae* was outside the pale of responsible Roman Catholic theological activity. Clearly, however, Professor Vaughan represented one of a variety of theological options on this matter. In addition to the expert testimony, the subject professors presented to the Inquiry Board accounts of the statements of certain national hierarchies and of various individual bishops in the United States and throughout the world, together with reports of the declarations and actions of overwhelmingly large numbers of distinguished American and European theologians, all of which upheld the possibility of dissent from the Encyclical. Professor Vaughan's testimony serves to indicate the manifest diversity of theological judgments on this issue within the pale of responsible Roman Catholic theological activity. The Inquiry Board thus had sufficient reason to reach a functional theological judgment, on an academic evaluation of the data presented, that dissent from a particular ethical conclusion of *Humanae Vitae* is within the pale of responsible Roman Catholic theological activity.

2) The Question of Public Dissent. Public manifestation of responsible dissent may, at times, be itself responsible Roman Catholic theological activity. It is true that theological "manuals" dating from the nineteeth century either limit dissent to private dissent or do not explicitly acknowledge the right to public dissent. However, the reasons themselves proposed by the manualists could call for public dissent in certain circumstances. Expert historical testimony given by Professor John T. Noonan, Jr., of the Law School of the University of California (Berkeley) indicates that in other historical cases of theological dissent the dissent was made public and communicated to the faithful who were affected by the teaching dissented from, *i.e.,* to those who had a right to knowledge of the dissent. Again, as set forth in detail in the companion volume, the contemporary theologian has a responsibility to many different constituencies who have a right to be informed of his theological judgments and interpretations: *e.g.,* the Church as a whole, the hierarchical magisterium itself, the people directly concerned with the matter in question, priests, non-Catholics, fellow academicians. In the present ecclesiological context with its stress on co-responsibility, it is within the pale of responsible Roman Catholic theology

to say that the theologian has an obligation to communicate his dissent to all who have a right to know it.

In the last few years the hierarchical magisterium and theologians have emphasized the right to know in the Church and need for a true public opinion in the Church. The Catholic Church in the twentieth century, like all contemporary mankind, is more acutely aware and conscious of the mass media of communication existing in the world today. The methods employed by both the Pope and hierarchies throughout the world made extensive use of press conferences and the mass media of communication. The 1968 Pastoral Letter of the American Bishops, *On Human Life in our Day,* acknowledges the legitimacy of public theological dissent, cautioning against scandal.

Even the one expert witness who disagreed with the position taken by the subject professors agreed that in this day and age the theologian has an obligation to use the mass media in some circumstances, even in the case of dissent. Professor Austin Vaughan, whose testimony was commissioned by the Inquiry Board to set forth a contrary theological position on the right to dissent in Catholic theology, agreed that there was no impropriety in the professors' "manner and mode" of dissent (assuming that the content of their statement was supportable). "My main problem is not manner or method. I think that a method that involves going to the press and television . . . if the issue is sufficiently important . . . is almost unavoidable and inescapable even if you don't go to them."

Public silence on the part of professors who "privately" dissent from authoritative, noninfallible teaching could be looked upon as irresponsible by many people in theological and academic circles, both Catholic and non-Catholic. The Encyclical itself, and the rumors preceding its release, were prominently mentioned and discussed on radio, television, and in newspapers and magazines. The news media were actively seeking out theologians for their opinions. Many people were directly affected by the teaching of the Encyclical and needed theological interpretation. Priests in their role as counsellors and confessors needed guidance. Non-

Catholics, both theologians and other interested people, were wondering what would be the Catholic reaction concerning the Encyclical.

President Bennett of Union Theological Seminary, an expert on AATS norms, also testified that, despite the assertion of the Trustees in their December 23 letter that many persons other than those within the Church questioned the propriety of the subject declarations and actions in terms of the norms of responsible academic procedure, he was aware only of praise for the subject declarations and actions in non-Catholic circles.

He testified that the concept of the responsibility of the theologians found in the prepared written testimony of the subject professors was an admirable formulation, and that theologians might be guilty of withdrawal from responsibility if they hesistated to make public a responsible theological point of view (within the context of their own faith commitment) merely because such point of view represented a challenge to traditional formulations. He thought that suppression of such public disagreement might lead to even more confusion than the statements made initiating the dialogue.

President Bennett further testified that the Statement by Catholic Theologians was enormously helpful to the Protestant community in mitigating the appearance of the Roman Catholic Church as a monolithic institution, and that, specifically, the dissent of professors at Catholic University has made a favorable impression of the University in ecumenical circles because it shows that there is academic freedom at the University, and that theologians at the University are able to speak as scholars and thinkers.

He also commented on the prepared testimony submitted by the subject professors on the question of their responsibility as theologians to the Church and to the academic communuity:

I have never known any Protestant to work it out quite so well, but I think it is a very good statement. This responsibility to speak to the church, whatever be the authority, and as well as the faithful as a community, the responsibility to speak to other churches and to the public and so on, I think is admirably spelled out.

In fact, I used it the other day. We were having a discussion of the role of the faculty and our students were on the warpath at the moment, and they wanted the professors to give all of their time to the students, and I used this illustration of how this professor had this other role which nobody else could fill of dealing with the church and the public and so on.

In the context of the theologians' manifold responsibilities, it would hardly be irresponsible or "beyond the pale of Catholic faith" for theologians to state their views candidly and publicly.

Professor Burghardt, as editor of a technical theology journal, affirmed that theologians were not to be limited to such narrow channels of expression on questions of broad public impact. He testified that the "actions" of the dissenting professors, in making their position public in a most effective way, were within the pale of responsible Catholic theological activity. He testified that the Statement by Catholic Theologians could not have been confined within technical theological journals (even if that approach had been attempted) given the current circumstances including subscription to theological journals by major news media and the popular interest in the Encyclical. Furthermore, he affirmed, even if dissent from the Encyclical *could* have been confined to technical theological journals, it should not have been. He testified that the theologian has a real relationship with the faithful Catholics which makes it necessary for him, with increasing frequency, to deal immediately with large groups of the faithful.

Professor Burghardt testified that, in view of the responsible reasons for a public response of theologians to the Encyclical, and in view of the three or four years of serious theological study and controversy that had been going on before the Encyclical was promulgated, the response set forth in the Statement by Catholic Theologians was not excessively quick in the circumstances, as some Catholic University Trustees apparently thought.

Expert testimony of Kenneth Woodward, Religion Editor, *Newsweek* magazine, supplemented Professor Burghardt's analysis of the propriety of the professors' manner and mode of dissent.

Mr. Woodward explained the methods and practices of the

religion department of *Newsweek* magazine in obtaining, formulating and selectively publicizing matters of general theological interest or concern. He testified that expert and representative theological views are actively and constantly solicited by his worldwide staff; that a large number of technical and semitechnical theological and religious periodicals are subscribed to and read by *Newsweek,* and that editors and publishers of scholarly theological works spontaneously supply him with advance notice or copies of "interesting" writings precisely so that they may be communicated popularly to the widest possible audience. He testified that it is virtually impossible today to conceal a significant theological view from the public; that a sudden "silence" by American theologians after the issuance of *Humanae Vitae* would have been inexplicable, and would have itself given rise to a *Newsweek* story speculating on the reasons for silence. He testified that large-scale "private" dissent on the part of American theologians from the specific ethical conclusions of the Encyclical would have quickly and inevitably become "public" in any event.

Over 700 American Catholic theologians in various statements and announcements publicly dissented in this case. Many of the most highly respected European theologians publicly dissented in a joint declaration. Testimony also was submitted to the Inquiry Board which showed the extent of public theological dissent in Europe, particularly West Germany. One could rightly characterize as "public dissent" some of the statements made by national groups of bishops such as the Belgians, French and Canadians.

Even the American bishops, as noted in chapter five, had in their 1968 Pastoral Letter acknowledged the legitimacy of at least scholarly dissent and had articulated broad norms for expressing such dissent publicly. Those broad statements seem to be guidelines about which all parties concerned would be in substantial agreement. These norms mentioned by the American bishops (presupposing well-founded reasons for dissent) can be reduced to the following:

1) They ["Norms of licit theological dissent"] require of him care-

ful respect for the consciences of those who lack his special competence or opportunity for judicious investigation. These norms also require setting forth his dissent with propriety and with regard for the gravity of the matter and the deference due the authority which pronounced on it.

2) The reverence due all sacred matters, particularly questions which touch on salvation, will not necessarily require the responsible scholar to relinquish his opinion but certainly to propose it with prudence born of intellectual grace and a Christian confidence that the truth is great and will prevail.

The expression of theological dissent . . . [must be] such as not to give scandal.

To the extent that certain of the bishops' prescriptions may be harmonized with AAUP's and AATS's principles of academic responsibility, they may serve as guides for evaluating the theologians' dissent. The bishops' norm can be classed in three particular categories:

a) *Respect for the Consciences of Others, Propriety and Due Deference for the Teaching Authority*: This standard clearly parallels AAUP's requirements of respect for the opinions of others. The interpretive development of this known norm is certainly germane to the application of the bishops' norms. It is clear, as the experts informed the Inquiry Board, that the theologians did not violate the AAUP norms; the facts show this conclusion to hold true even in the bishops' context.

The Statement by Theologians of July 30 begins: "As Roman Catholic theologians we respectfully acknowledge a distinct role of hierarchical magisterium (teaching office) in the Church of Christ." Newspapers frequently cited the professors as saying their declarations and actions were neither a rebellion nor an uprising. The major thrust of the position taken by the subject professors was that one could be a loyal Catholic with true Catholic respect for the Pope and still dissent from the absolute ban on artificial contraception contained in the Encyclical—one can dissent and still not resign from the Church or from any office in the Church.

Under the heading of propriety or respect for the opinions of others, one could also consider the allegation that the subject professors apparently undertook to organize public opposition to the Papal teaching. The word "organize" has many different connotations. The Inquiry Board specifically inquired as to whether any undue force or pressure was used to induce other theologians to subscribe to the Statement of July 30, and they did not discover even the hint of such pressure.

The subject professors could not be said to have "organized opposition to the teaching of the Pope" as those terms are generally understood. As detailed in the companion volume, Roman Catholic theology has always attributed theological importance and significance to the number of theologians who maintain a certain position. As an academician, the theologian is conscious of the need to consult with his peers about his own opinions. As a Roman Catholic theologian, he is aware that the number of theologians holding a particular judgment has importance both in the theological and the practical order. In moral theology, the number of theologians maintaining a particular judgment furnishes sufficient weight for a person to safely follow that judgment in his actions ("probabilism"). As a prudent person, the Roman Catholic theologian also realizes the added weight given to a judgment because of the stature and number of qualified people who adhere to it.

From the viewpoint of Roman Catholic theology (even as specified in the bishops' 1968 Pastoral Letter) and AAUP's standard of appropriate restraint, there is no impropriety in the manner, style and method in which the subject professors expressed their dissent publicly. Expert theological witnesses, including Professor Vaughan, who could not accept the position proposed by the subject professors, saw no impropriety in the manner, style and method of the actions of the professors. Similar manners, styles, and methods have been employed by other groups of American and foreign Roman Catholic theologians both in the instance of the response to *Humanae Vitae* and in other cases.

b) *Scandal.* AAUP has rejected scandal as an applicable standard of academic responsibility in the *Caldwell* case. In that case, however, the term was used in the broad sense, as a standard of conduct clearly objectionable as hopelessly vague, going quite beyond the Roman Catholic faith-commitment. But the bishops must be considered as referring to scandal in the proper *theological sense*. As explained more fully in the companion volume, scandal, strictly so-called, is a technical theological term classically defined as a word or deed, evil or at least with the appearance of evil, which furnishes to another an occasion of sin. Thus scandal in the strict sense exists only when the act or word itself is evil or has the appearance of evil and is an occasion for leading others into sin. The declarations and actions of the subject professors, since they are within the pale of responsible Roman Catholic theological options, cannot constitute scandal in the strict sense of the term.

The looser and nontechnical use of the term scandal is understood as the wonder or questioning which arises among people because of an unaccustomed action, without anyone's being enticed to sin (although such wonderment may constitute for some persons an obstacle, at least temporarily, to the smooth development of their Christian lives). However, the fact that such wonderment or questioning might arise in a particular case is not of itself a convincing reason for not acting. This consideration logically leads to the norm that the public theological dissent must be proposed *prudently*.

(c) *Prudence*. Prudence is practical wisdom which must weigh all the pertinent factors involved before arriving at a conclusion. In complex human questions there will always be some negative effects resulting from one's actions. It is inhuman and contrary to reality to think that one cannot act if there may be some negative effect coming from one's actions. The closest AAUP analog to this standard is obviously the requirement of "appropriate restraint."

As explained more fully in the companion volume, public dissent is not prudent or appropriate in every situation. All the pertinent elements must be taken into consideration, weighed and balanced. In the present case, for the reasons mentioned above, public dissent was clearly not imprudent or a violation of AAUP's canons of appropriate restraint, which is concerned solely with the *manner* of public expression, and not the substance.

It is true that the declarations and actions of the subject professors did occasion some wonderment and questioning among some Catholic people. But much greater harm could have resulted if the theologians had not made their dissent public. According to expert testimony, Professor Burghardt's in particular, many other people—concerned spouses, priests, non-Catholics and even the theologians themselves—would have suffered harm if the dissent were not made public. In commenting upon the wonderment or questioning occasioned by the declaration and actions of the subject professors, it should be recalled that many others in the Church acted in the same way. The fact that so many responsible people from throughout the entire world reacted in a similar way is a convincing corroboration of the prudence of such actions and declarations.

Under the norm of prudence, one might raise the charge about "quickness" of the response made by the theologians. However, the subject professors had long been familiar with the moral issues involved in artificial contraception and found in *Humanae Vitae* no argumentation which had not already been thoroughly evaluated by the theological community. They were qualified to respond adequately at that time, and there was an urgent situation that called for a prompt response. AAUP's standard of "appropriate restraint" does not admit of questions about the time and place of expression. To AAUP, quickness can only be related to the academic competence, such as if the statement were so hastily drawn as to be professionally unsupportable. But in this case, there has never been any real question but that the dissenting statement was from its inception supportable within the academic discipline it purported to deal with: *Roman Catholic* theology. In view of all the factors involved, the public dissent of the subject professors followed one of the possible responsible prudential options open to Catholic theologians in the circumstances.

The dissenting theologians realized that their declarations and actions had caused difficulty and confusion among some people

in the Roman Catholic Church. Most complex human actions do
have such negative effects, but, under the norm of prudence, one
may not refrain from action merely because he foresees some
negative consequences—all pertinent factors must be taken into
consideration. The Inquiry Board directed a number of questions
to expert witnesses and to the professors themselves about this
question of the overall balance of the effects of the Statement of
dissent. During the questioning of Professor Hunt, the Chairman of the Inquiry Board, with some hesitancy, mentioned a
"colloquy" that had been reported to him and to another member
of the Board as having occurred at the August 18-19, 1968, meeting at the Statler-Hilton Hotel in New York. In that reported
colloquy, Professor Hunt, in response to the question "Were you
not concerned that the Statement by theologians would introduce
confusion among the laity?", was said to have responded that
part of the purpose of the Statement was to "create confusion."

Professor Hunt asked the Chairman for the source of the reputed
colloquy. The Inquiry proceeding went "off the record" momen-
tarily. When the recorded testimony was resumed, the Inquiry
Board Chairman stated that the report of the colloquy came
to his attention and to the attention of a fellow Board member
from a source of information which "originated with a statement
of Bishop Wright." Professor Hunt testified that the report of the
colloquy was "utterly false." He said that Professor Curran had
indeed addressed the question of "confusion" at the Statler-Hilton
meeting. Professor Curran was recalled to testify. He set forth
the context of his remarks on the evening of August 18 which
made clear that he had spoken of confusion as an unfortunately
necessary result of informing the laity of their right to dissent. He
related that Bishop Wright interrupted him to ask: "Are you
saying that you deliberately caused confusion among the faithful?"
Professor Curran further testified that he (Professor Curran) and
others at the meeting, especially Professors Hunt and Maguire,
had called the participants' attention (immediately after Bishop
Wright's question) to the context of Professor Curran's remarks.
Professor Curran testified that the subject of confusion was not

mentioned again that evening, and that, since Bishop Wright had announced that he would not attend the August 19 session, the subject did not come up again at the Statler-Hilton meeting. Professor Curran testified that neither he, Professor Hunt, nor any other dissenter ever admitted an intention to "create confusion" or ever had such an intention.

The record laid before the Board of Inquiry and now available to the entire educational community, therefore makes clear that the theologians' "extramural," dissent with intramural effects violated neither the norms of expression generally accepted in the American academic community nor the norms specifying professional competence of teachers of Roman Catholic theology—and these are the *only* standards which such dissent must satisfy. Furthermore, their dissent did not violate the later announced norms proposed by the American bishops.

10

The Inquiry:
A Further Issue of Responsible
Academic Procedure—The Trustees'
Threat of Suspension

"I am not an important person. I have no international rep-utation to uphold. But there are thousands or we could consider millions of people who are making a judgment on us, a harsh judgment, and this puts a pall over our whole work. The whole proceedings are causing a great stress on our actual perfor-mance and it has been caused, frankly, by the appeal of the Board [of Trustees] to the procedures regarding suspension and the conditions under which we were made to continue working here this term."—Professor Warren Reich, one of the "subject professors," testifying on the effect of the Inquiry and Suspension, January 10, 1969.

The Trustees, in the December 23 letter, asked the Inquiry Board to recommend how the faculty, the Board of Trustees and the University as a whole could "best accomplish, in the present instance and for the future, their common tasks of advancing authentic intellectual investigation and of demonstrating in action their promise of fidelity to the teachings of the Catholic Church." In the context of this request to the Inquiry Board, the subject professors and their counsel also asked the Board to examine the conduct of the Trustees in threatening to suspend the dissenting professors as leverage to enforce an unacceptable condition of silence.

The conflict between the professors and the Trustees concerning the suspension-or-silence condition proposed by the Trustees on September 5 had been simmering throughout the course of the Inquiry proceedings. As of September 13, 1968, the professors had reached an agreement with Acting Rector Whalen which provided for neither silence nor suspension as the Trustees had proposed. However, the professors were surprised to learn in mid-November that Trustee Krol, the Cardinal-Archbishop of Philadelphia, apparently was under the impression that the professors had been silenced. The parents of one of the professors had heard Cardinal Krol's pastoral letter of November 19 read in their Church accusing their son of unprecedented conduct which put the loyalty of the faithful to a cruel test, and stating as a fact that their son and the other dissenting Catholic University professors were not to have been allowed back into the classroom unless they agreed to cease their public dissent.

Proceeding from this knowledge, the subject professors were able to learn of Acting Rector Whalen's "Special Communication" to the American bishops which informed them on September 18 (just five days after the University administration had agreed to qualify materially the Trustees' conditions) that the professors had agreed to the conditions of silence outlined by the Trustees on September 5. This communication may have misled Cardinal Krol. Indeed, one of the professors was at that time busy with final preparation of his book affirming the dissenting position of the theologians respecting *Humanae Vitae,* with the full knowledge of the University administration. Finally, the professors learned from the last paragraph of the December 23 letter, that the Board of Trustees itself was misinformed about the University administration's acquiescence in the professors' refusal to accept the condition of silence proposed by the Trustees: that paragraph expressed the Trustees' "appreciation of the ready and gracious acceptance" of the condition of silence. Thus, when

Bishop Shannon appeared to testify before the Inquiry Board on January 10, there was an apparent factual dispute between the professors and the Trustees concerning whether or not the professors had in fact agreed to abstain from their public dissent to the Encyclical or whether they had agreed, as the University press release of September 13 stated, to accept the applicability of the Trustees' conditions only insofar as they proved in any instance to be compatible with generally accepted norms of academic freedom and responsibility. The professors understood that the governing AAUP principles of academic freedom in fact prevented any application of the Trustees' conditions.

More importantly, however, when it became clear that the Trustees were not going to make charges against the professors, the threat of suspension lost any color of procedural justification under the norms of AAUP. On September 5, the Trustees had made their threat of suspension "in accord with" a specific AAUP norm (which they cited, by page number, in their press release). The December 23 letter asserted that the Trustees' purpose in threatening to suspend or silence the dissenting professors was "to create a climate within which the Inquiry could be conducted with charity, clarity and out of the heat of controversy." AAUP does not sanction any charitable suspension for the purpose of avoiding controversy. AAUP permits suspension, as a general matter, only when charges respecting fitness to teach are pending against a professor and "only if immediate harm to himself or others is threatened by his continuance" (*AAUP 1958 Statement on Procedural Standards in Faculty Dismissal Proceedings*, para. 3). Exceptions to the rule that charges must be pending are allowed in cases of immediate physical danger caused by what AAUP officials have termed situations of "leprosy or lunacy," that is, mental or physical conditions such that the present danger to the student in the classroom would be patently unavoidable if the teacher were allowed to remain in his post pending a protracted hearing process. Consequently, the Trustees' threat of suspension was not only a violation of academic freedom (as the professors perceived in refusing to accede to the conditions of silence proposed) but also a violation of responsible academic procedure. Indeed, many of the witnesses during the Inquiry testified to that effect.

On January 10, once Bishop Shannon had made clear that the Trustees meant to make no charges, counsel for the professors demanded that the Trustees, consistent with their affirmation of the principles of responsible academic procedure and with their citation of the AAUP norm on suspension, retract or rescind their threat. Bishop Shannon, however, took the position that the Trustees did "not cite the AAUP procedures as the directive for [their] action. . . ." Counsel for the professors objected that the Trustees were using "a reference to the AAUP to create a patina of academic due process . . . [merely to] keep up the image of the University for the sake of its exterior relations in the academic world, and this nation. . . ." The Chairman of the Inquiry Board pointed out that the professors had not in fact been suspended. Counsel for the professors recalled, however, that that fact was due to the agreement about the alternative condition of silence worked out with Acting Rector Whalen: "All of these men resumed their teaching duties at the commencement of the term, after extended negotiations . . . in which [the Acting Rector] was advised that [the Trustees' condition of silence] violated our rights of academic freedom [and] in which we worked out a stipulation which emasculated these conditions in effect by stipulating that they were to be interpreted and applied in accordance with [AAUP norms]." Moreover, counsel for the professors affirmed that the mere threat of suspension (with its direct reference to AAUP procedures) was itself a violation of their academic rights, because of the common understanding in the academic world that those who are threatened with AAUP-sanctioned suspension are subject to grave charges of professional misconduct. Thus, since the Trustees made no charges, they had put the professors under an unjustified professional cloud by their threat of suspension adverting to AAUP procedures. Academic counsel for the professors particularly emphasized the serious light in which the academic community views a suspension:

I have been involved in AAUP investigations in which suspension was at issue, immediate suspension for a trip to Cuba. It was the unanimous and immediate opinion of the [AAUP] investigative committee that this suspension was unjustified because there was no business in pleading danger to the institution from the bad reputation that it would get in its community because a member of its faculty had been to Cuba.

The only basis for it would have been in the case of gross moral turpitude, or some case of a sort where the students were directly threatened by the continuance of that person in the classroom.

We were convinced, and I think I would be speaking now for general academic opinion, that the most serious sanction that can be brought against a member of the faculty is to be suspended from his teaching duty, to be denied access to his students, and to have this even threatened, as it is here, [subject to] conditions put to him, seems to me to be bringing, as I see it, *de facto* charges whether they are there or not.

It was unnecessary to make that [threat of suspension]; it was gratuitous; it is bringing a huge piece of artillery to bear on a quite irrelevant point, it seems.

Bishop Shannon, despite his insistence that the Trustees did not mean to use AAUP norms as a directive for their threat of suspension, adverted to the AAUP suspension rubric which allows such action "if immediate harm to himself or others is threatened." Bishop Shannon informed the Inquiry Board that the Trustees read this standard as requiring a showing of "possible harm" and suggested that one such possible harm to which the suspension threat was addressed was "precipitous action by a member of the Board." (The only logical interpretation of this otherwise unexplained reference seems to be that certain members of the Board, who as bishops have canonical jurisdiction over certain of the professors might otherwise have exercised their ecclesiastical power to remove the dissenters from their teaching positions.)

Counsel for the professors reiterated that the Trustees, whatever their intention, should not be permitted to "have it both ways" under AAUP norms—that is, make a threat of suspension but not make charges prerequisite to that threat. Since no charges were to be made, counsel urged that the Trustees clarify the record and reputation of the professors by withdrawing their threat of suspension, publicly.

Bishop Shannon questioned whether the professors had actually been harmed by the Trustees' threat but agreed to convey the professors' counsel's views to the Trustees. One of the subject professors, Warren Reich, took the floor and assured Bishop Shannon that the professors' counsel were accurately portraying the burdensome effects which the Trustees' threat of suspension had on the professors during the course of the Inquiry:

PROFESSOR REICH: After a long discussion this afternoon, Bishop, you said although you didn't completely agree with our attorney, you were available to be of help to us as individuals. I would like to speak as a human being and as an individual who is not only a professor but concerned about the conditions under which I work.

I just want you to know that they are almost unbearable. A real injustice has been done already. It is an unworkable situation. I think the words of Professor Webb, who is very highly regarded, this afternoon are very important about using a cannon to attack a small problem. I am not an important person. I have no international reputation to uphold. But there are thousands or we could consider millions of people who are making a judgment on us, a harsh judgment, and this puts a pall over our whole work. The whole proceedings are causing a great stress on our actual performance and it has been caused, frankly, by the appeal of the Board to the procedures regarding suspension and the conditions under which we were made to continue working here this term.

I just want to say, as an individual, that this is very important, rather than thinking it is only our attorney—I think I am speaking for others, too—that there is a real hardship under which we are working and we feel it should be reversed, I feel it should be reversed.

BISHOP SHANNON: I accept that, Father, and you can trust that I will take that sentiment to the Board and I would prepare a copy of that statement if you can give it to me as Father gave it. Thank you.

Nothing further was heard from Bishop Shannon, however, on the subject of the suspension.

By letter dated January 16, 1968, the professors' counsel requested the Trustees to rescind their threat of suspension since it was inconsistent with the Trustees' expressed commitment to the accepted norms of responsible academic procedure in American universities. The professors through their counsel also requested the Academic Senate to reconvene its "Committee A" charged with interpreting the terms of the agreement which the professors had reached with the University regarding the Trustees' proposed condition of silence in lieu of suspension. That Committee, upon investigation, refuted the Trustees' claim that the professors had accepted their conditions of silence, concluding that those conditions were never efficacious within the University community and that it was understood by all that the professors agreed only to maintain public silence concerning the Inquiry proceedings pending issuance of the Inquiry Report. Committee A directed, and the Academic Senate agreed, that a public statement be made to that effect by the University. No such statement was made.

Counsel for the professors in their proposed findings also urged the Inquiry Board to consider not only the academic responsibility of the professors but also the propriety of the Trustees' action of September 5, particularly their action threatening suspension. During the Inquiry, testimony was elicited from President Cross of Hunter College that the invocation of the AAUP suspension clause "would create a very serious cloud about the reputation of the individual concerned," and that such a serious cloud should not be put upon any professor without a prior, thorough investigation by professional peers. He affirmed that the suspension device was not meant to be used in cases of intellectual differences of opinion and that "if suspension is used in anything except the most extraordinary circumstances, the whole climate of freedom seems to be very seriously impaired."

President Yanitelli testified that he could not understand or concur in the actions of the Catholic University Trustees on September 5, both ordering the Inquiry and invoking the AAUP suspension clause against the dissenting professors. He saw no grounds for either action, especially in light of the identical declarations and actions with respect to the Encyclical on the part of faculty members at his own college. He had already explained that he had resisted external pressures to compromise the academic freedom of his university's theologians through such devices as burdensome inquiries or unwarranted suspensions. The Trustees' invocation of suspension was to President Yanitelli "putting the cart before the horse. I feel that first you get your evidence and then you move."

11

The Report of the Faculty
Board of Inquiry

*"The 30 July statement of the subject professors represents
a responsible theological dissent from the teaching of the Encyclical 'Humanae Vitae' and this dissent is reasonably supported as a tenable scholarly position."—Conclusion 1, Report
of The Catholic University of America Faculty Board of Inquiry, April 1, 1969.*

After the professors had submitted their proposed findings (neither
the party representing the Trustees, nor their counsel, submitted
proposed findings), the Inquiry Board on the afternoon of April
1, 1969, submitted its Report to the University Academic Senate.

The Inquiry Report concluded that "the declarations and actions
of the subject professors with respect to the papal encyclical *Humanae Vitae* did not violate any of their obligations to Catholic
University . . . , did not offend against responsible academic procedure and did not depart from the spirit of the University."[1]

The Inquiry Board recommended that no further proceedings
be initiated which would question the dissenting professors' "fitness to teach." The Report specifically affirmed the applicability
of the "norms of responsible academic conduct generally accepted
by American universities," found no need to vary those norms in
the case of theologians at a Catholic university, and proceeded to
apply those norms to determine, within the framework of AAUP's
recognized grounds, whether there was any reason to question
the subject professors' fitness to teach. In applying these norms to

152

the total context of activity surrounding the Inquiry, the Report found much fault with the actions of the Chancellor and the Trustees but none with the declarations and actions of the dissenting professors.

The Report's conclusions respecting the professors can be grouped under three general headings, corresponding to the permissible grounds for questioning fitness to teach: professional incompetence, dereliction of duty, and violation of the norms of extramural expression.

Professional Incompetence

As a preliminary matter, the Board of Inquiry reached the requisite functional judgment with respect to the tenability of the theological position taken by the dissenting professors in their Statement of dissent, *i.e.,* that "spouses may responsibly decide in accordance with their conscience that artificial contraception in some circumstances is permissible and indeed necessary to promote and foster the values and sacredness of marriage":

It is not within the competence or the mandate of the Board to judge the theological correctness or incorrectness of the position taken in the statement. However . . . it is the conclusion of the Board that the statement expresses a tenable theological opinion.

In fact, the first recommendation of the Report was that the University "recognize that the commentary made by the subject professors in their July 30, 1968, statement is adequately supported by theological scholarship . . . ." The Report recited the evidence it considered most persuasive in upholding the tenability, and hence the "competence," of the theologians' declaration of dissent.

From the classical instances of major, discernible change in the teaching of the hierarchical magisterium, such as the teachings on interest-taking, religious freedom and biblical science, it is clear that noninfallible pronouncements are reversible. It is not pertinent whether the change takes place because of theological reflection and publication, the words or actions of the members of the Church who are not theologians, or intrinsic factors in human society: the fact of such change means that the door to theological inquiry is not closed.

There has been an explicit and formal recognition of the right to dissent from noninfallible teaching, although couched in limited terms, even in the common teaching of theologians prior to the Second Vatican Council, that is, during the post-Tridentine period when the likelihood of such dissent was considered remote. (Cf. the theological manuals enumerated and cited in the prepared testimony.)

The right to dissent in such cases has been most recently acknowledged by the National Conference of Catholic Bishops in the pastoral statement already mentioned.

Finally, attention should be given to the arguments advanced concerning the usefulness of dissent by theologians within the Church community: it is a means of informing the sense of the faithful and of hastening the legitimate development of doctrine; it is a means of correcting a noninfallible statement and thus strengthening and supporting the continuity of the hierarchical magisterium; in Catholic doctrine it may be regarded as a working of the Spirit in the Church.

It is evident that theologians other than the professors have publicly dissented in greater or less degree, in accord with the above concept of the theologian's office, from the papal teaching in the encyclical *Humanae Vitae*. In particular, there were the other signatories of the statement, principally members of the Catholic Theological Society of America and the College Theology Society, as well as individual theologians and groups of theologians in various countries. The several statements of the episcopal magisterium in other countries, which included interpretations differing in some measure from the encyclical and which were based upon theological data, may also be mentioned.

The Pastoral statement of the National Conference of Catholic Bishops, *Human Life in Our Day* (November, 1968,) issued after the Encyclical *Humanae Vitae*, recognizes the right of theologians to dissent from noninfallible teaching and takes into account the contemporary circumstances which may affect the public expression of that dissent.

The Board feels that specific reference should be made to the several publics to which the professors felt responsible as theologians, according to their own statement: (a) to the whole Church; (b) to the pope and the other bishops; (c) to their fellow theologians; (d) to the individuals touched by the contraception issue; (e) to the priests of the United States, including former students; (f) to the University community; (g) to the public communications media; (h) to non-Catholics, especially those already engaged in dialogue; (i) to men of good will, to whom *Humanae Vitae* was addressed.

The Board then reaches its conclusion as to this matter that:

. . . The Board has received substantial evidence of the seriousness of the theological endeavor in which the professors engaged and of the professors' consciousness of their pastoral obligation as theologians.

Acknowledging the legitimacy of theological dissent by way of evaluation and interpretation of noninfallible teachings of the hierarchical magisterium and in the light of the above considerations, the Board recognizes the right of the professors to act as they did, in their capacity of Roman Catholic theologians, and it accepts their conviction that they had a duty so to act. It therefore finds that the professors acted responsibly as theologians.

Dereliction of Duty

The Inquiry Board made clear that the professors' dissent had not violated any "valid and currently enforceable" Statute or bylaw of the University or other sources of specific obligations of the subject professors. The Inquiry Report noted that copies of the University's existing Statutes were not readily available and that, in some degree, the existing Statutes "are inconsistent with modern American practice in higher education." The Report particularly took to task the procedures set forth in Article 66:

. . . Article 66 provides that an alleged "offense against Catholic Doctrine" would be submitted to three Bishops for investigation and final adjudication, whereas all modern procedural standards provide for investigation by academic peers.

The Inquiry Board's Report rejected any application of any Statute of the University inconsistent with the maximum restraints on expression set forth in the 1940 Statement of AAUP, and made clear that charges may be filed only if "the extramural utterances 'raised grave doubts concerning the faculty member's fitness for his position.'"

The Trustees had cited the Profession of Faith taken by Catholic professors of theology, among others, in virtue of canon 1405 of the Code of Canon Law and Article 50 of the Statutes as a basis for some of their questions. The Report considered whether any question was raised by the dissent with respect to the profession of faith.

It is evident that the profession of faith made by professors of theology differs in no way from the profession made by other believing Roman Catholics.

In the formula for the profession of faith, a distinction is made between the Nicene-Constantinopolitan Creed, which is explicitly made the object of divine faith, and the additional text which is introduced: "I also embrace and retain . . . ." In this added text the expression, "as proposed by the Church," illustrates the precise issue already discussed, namely, the potential area for permitted dissent, for cause, from noninfallible teachings.

There is no incompatibility between the formula of assent to Catholic teachings and the declaration of the Second Vatican Council (Constitution on the Church, n. 25) concerning religious assent, in that "each and every thing" commands varying degrees of consideration, as this has been explained . . . in the light of the conciliar development of its own text.

The Board therefore finds that the professors in no way violated the professions of faith.

Norms of Extramural Expression (Paragraph (c) of AAUP 1940 Statement)

The Report considered, as the Trustees had directed:

Whether the style, mode and manner of the statement itself exceeded the bounds of academic propriety?

Whether the mode and manner of the release of the statement to the public was not in accord with responsible academic procedure as practiced in American universities?

These two questions were addressed under the familiar language of the 1940 Statement of AAUP.

The college or university teacher . . . should at all times be accurate, should exercise appropriate restraint, should show respect for the opinions of others, and should make every effort to indicate that he is not an institutional spokesman. . . .

The Board found that the style, mode and manner of the Statement of dissent "did not exceed the bounds of academic propriety":

The language of the July 30 Statement, in the judgment of the Board of Inquiry, was dignified, grave and measured. Its dignity was appropriate to the priestly office held by most of the subscribers; its gravity adapted to the seriousness of the papal document involved; and its avoidance of emotional connotations, prudently directed to the information of the public with the least possible confusion. In comparison with some other public criticisms of the encyclical, it reveals itself as a temperate expression. It respectfully acknowledged both the distinct role of hierarchical magisterium and the positive values concerning marriage contained in the encyclical. The Statement was published as the expression of a group of Roman Catholic theologians, and indication of the subscribers' institutional connections was given in the commonly accepted manner merely as a means of identification. The testimony of expert witnesses from other American educational institutions, both Catholic and secular, who appeared before the Inquiry Board, upheld the subject professors' view that they had made every reasonable effort to avoid labelling the Statement as a Catholic University position.

The Board of Inquiry, with respect to the timing of the release, found that the subject professors "acted responsibly and in accord with American university practice":

The statement was released within a very short time after the publication of the encyclical. The question of the propriety of this suddenness has been raised. There are circumstances, however, to be considered. As already mentioned, the controversy was by no means new.

Moreover, it was an important issue, and even those who are not moral theologians in the strict sense had had full opportunity and incentive to inform themselves and to take some position on the issue. The encyclical's teaching on artificial contraception purported to be and was in fact essentially the same teaching with which the theologians were familiar before the appearance of the encyclical. The theologians were careful to read the document before framing their statement. It should also be noted that had the theologians withheld or delayed their announcement, reporters would have sought their interpretations, as happened elsewhere. It is at least possible that any statements would have been issued with less opportunity for careful preparation and with much less control over the conditions of their release.

The Board found that the theologians' use of public media was no "departure from accepted standards of responsible academic procedure as practiced in American universities":

> It is common academic practice to use all effective and rational means of publication and discussion. The dissemination of information and opinion in various ways is the most general service which the university performs for the public. The practice is encouraged by leaders outside the universities, including churchmen. Responsible dissemination to an appropriate audience is meant to improve the quality of information and understanding concerning religious issues.
> Moreover, as already mentioned, the dissemination of the theologians' views through the public media was unavoidable. The press and television in America do not wait for news to come to them, but instead go to experts when this is appropriate. In the present instance the press and television took the initiative in trying to elicit statements from the theologians. The latter, for their part, showed professional restraint by refusing to make a statement until they had read the document and talked over their own response to it.
> Furthermore, it is unrealistic to suppose that all theological discussion of the issue could have been withheld from the public media, even if this were desirable. No one seems to argue for this position. On the other hand, any attempt to present only "approved" theological interpretations would have been contrived and even ominous, and would have strained the credibility of those who had already followed

the controversy through the same public media. When controversy has been open, dissent inevitably becomes public.

The Board of Inquiry found "nothing exceptional in the organized preparation and release" of the Statement:

Statements sponsored by a group are a common feature of American life, especially among academics. Those who read newspapers and watch television are familiar with such releases. The Board does not see any significance in the fact that the statement was prepared and issued by many together rather than by each separately. To contravene the standards of good academic practice the organizers would have had to use methods contrary to the spirit of academic life, such as pressure of one kind or another, the fraudulent use of names, misrepresentation of the position, or recruitment of incompetent signers. The Board could find no evidence of any such violations.

There was no evidence of pressure. Some who were not approached initiated the approach themselves. Others were not accepted because they were not competent in the appropriate fields or because they had not read the encyclical.

In the testimony elicited by the Board it became clear that each signer had responsible grounds and signed within his competency. Not everyone was a theologian in the strict sense, and it might have been preferable had the subscribers referred to themselves by a broader term; however, those who were not theologians were competent to render a professional opinion on the issue. It is possible, too, that the process of organization may have produced a more accurate statement.

It may be readily agreed that the joint statement had greater impact. However, if the promulgation of the statement is itself within the permissible norms of academic procedure, it would be absurd to demand that it be promulgated as ineffectively as possible.

The Board of Inquiry found that any use by the theologians of the University's name or facilities "was well within accepted American academic practice."

It was clear from the nature of the theologians' dissent that they were not speaking for the official hierarchical church. No one was found who thought the statement of the theologians was the official position of the university. Newspaper coverage consistently used Catholic

University as a means of identification only. Moreover, the presence of other institutional names on the full list made it even clearer that the institutional names were for identification only. As far as the Board of Inquiry knows, no other governing board has taken any action on the basis of such an alleged confusion. Finally, the Board of Inquiry is satisfied that the theologians took every reasonable precaution in the circumstances to avoid such a confusion.

In the context of its application of norms of responsible academic procedure, the Inquiry Board recognized that certain of the allegations made against the dissenters at the Trustees' meeting of September 5 were false. In this regard the Inquiry Report called specific attention to Chancellor O'Boyle's reference to a statement he attributed to two of the subject professors "as though the statement of the professors . . . had actually appeared in several newspapers," when in fact it had never been made, let alone quoted in the press.

The Inquiry Report also severely criticized the Trustees for invoking the AAUP suspension clause without a hearing. The Report recommended that the Trustees give assurances they would not repeat such an action.

This Board finds that the actions of the Trustees on 5 September, in threatening suspension of subject professors and in giving public circulation of this threat, may have seriously damaged the academic standing of the professors, have certainly impaired the reputation of the academic departments concerned and, in some circles, have tarnished the reputation of the University. Even recognizing the "danger of immediate harm" rule, it appears to the Board that it is essential that the elements of academic due process should have been invoked and the threat of suspension should never have been made a matter of public knowledge. The seriousness was compounded by Rector Whalen's request to subject professors to sign a statement regarding opposition to the Encyclical and the obligation to silence, even though this request was later withdrawn.

The Board recommends that assurance be given the academic community of this university that, before even the process leading to the possibility of suspension or dismissal is initiated, such preliminary decision will be subject to due process and to the prior judgment of academic peers.

The Inquiry Report also expressed its affirmation of the existing norms of licit dissent.

Although the current inquiry was the result of a specific instance of dissent, it should be realized that it is inevitable that such instances will arise, rather frequently, in any university worthy of the name. The Board recommends as the basic norms of academic freedom to be observed in such cases:

a) 1940 Statement of Principles on Academic Freedom and Tenure, of the AAUP;

b) 1958 Statement on Procedural Standards in Faculty Dismissal Proceedings, of the AAUP;

c) 1964 Statement of Committee A on Extramural Utterances, of the AAUP;

d) 1967 Report and Draft Recommendation of a Special Committee on Academic Freedom in Church-related Colleges and Universities, of the AAUP.

The Board has considered other formulations, similar both in content and scope, of these norms (such as those of the ACLU, the AAU, the IFCU, etc.), but is of the opinion that careful adherence to the norms listed above would be adequate.

The 1960 norms of the American Association of Theological Schools, which incorporate the AAUP 1940 norms for academic freedom, and which consider both classroom teaching and extramural expression, are the most suitable norms currently available to academic institutions at which theology is taught. These norms provide adequate guides for specifying the grounds of alleged professional incompetence with respect to theology and other sacred sciences by reference to the confessional commitment of the particular school.

If the professional competence of a teacher of Roman Catholic theology is seriously questioned (whether on grounds of deviation from the Roman Catholic faith commitment, or on any other scholarly grounds), the presumptive judgment regarding the teacher's fitness for his position must be the province of his academic peers, made under conditions which assure academic due process. The Trustees should attach such weight to this judgment as is set forth in the AAUP 1958 Statement of Procedural Standards in Faculty Dismissal Proceedings.

A determination of doctrinal orthodoxy may, under AATS norms, be made by a public ecclesiastical tribunal. When such a determination is made, it is still for the academic community to render judgment concerning competency to teach.

No grounds other than fitness to teach . . . may be invoked as grounds for dismissal proceedings. As applied to extramural utterances the [1964] Statement on the subject is the best available and is fully adequate. . . .

No special norms are required because of the pontifical character of the University or of any of its Schools. The commitment of the Roman Catholic teacher in a pontifical university or school to the Catholic faith differs in no way whatever from the commitment of a Roman Catholic teacher in any other institution. The profession of Catholic faith and the context of the faith commitment are not affected by the canonical status of the institution.

The Inquiry Report also focused on a problem which had cast a shadow on the proceedings from their very commencement The priest-theologian is invariably subject to the ecclesiastical jurisdiction of a particular bishop or a particular religious superior and, if recalled from a university by his ecclesiastical superior because of his exercise of academic freedom, he would be faced with a barbarous conflict of conscience. Significantly, in their September 5 press release the Trustees stated that they recognized that "canonical decisions involving teachers of sacred sciences belong properly to the bishops of the Church." The Inquiry Board addressed itself to this subject in its Report when it said that in its opinion the ideal of academic freedom in situations involving clerics teaching sacred sciences requires "an understanding, in the form of contractual agreements if necessary, that such rights [of jurisdiction over priests] not be exercised outside responsible academic procedure."

Note

1. The full text of the Inquiry Report is on file in the Archives of the Catholic University of America.

12

Review and Decision:
The Trustees' Acceptance
of the Inquiry Report

*"The Board of Trustees accept the report of the Faculty
Board of Inquiry insofar as it pertains to the academic pro-
priety of the conduct of [the dissenting] faculty members."—
Statement of the Board of Trustees of the Catholic University
of America Concerning the Report of the Faculty Board of
Inquiry, June 15, 1969.*

The Academic Senate of Catholic University unanimously approved the Inquiry Report on April 1, and forwarded it to the
Acting Rector to be transmitted forthwith to the Trustees for
consideration at their April 12-13 meeting in Houston, Texas.
Copies of the Inquiry Report were also made available to the
subject professors and their counsel, with the understanding that
they would treat the Report as a confidential matter until the
Trustees had considered it. The Inquiry Report was mailed to all
the Trustees immediately by the University administration. A copy
of the Inquiry Report was also delivered through University channels to the Apostolic Delegate's Office in Washington, D.C. The
Academic Senate had not directed the latter action.

The Academic Senate had directed the Acting Rector to release
the Inquiry Report to the communications media upon the conclusion of the Trustees' meeting in Houston, regardless of the Trustees' disposition of the Report. A special public relations counsel

retained by the Chairman of the Board of Trustees contacted the professors and their civil counsel and informed them that the Chairman considered the treatment of the Inquiry Report "a moment of truth" for the University and that the Chairman of the Board was prepared to sacrifice unanimity on the Board for the sake of the principles of academic freedom affirmed in the Report. The public relations counsel noted, however, that it would be prudent for the professors, once the Report was released, not to "flaunt" its findings, particularly by calling attention to the inconsistency between the Report's conclusion that dissent from the Encyclical was a tenable theological position within the Roman Catholic faith commitment and the actions of Cardinal O'Boyle, the Archbishop of Washington, D.C., in suspending, in varying degrees, the pastoral faculties of those members of his archdiocesan clergy who indicated they would respect the dissenting position on the Encyclical. The professors and their counsel responded that they would not hold themselves to such restrictions, since they would amount to a forfeiture of the academic freedoms they had fought for and won in the Inquiry.

At the Trustees' meeting in Houston, the three identifiable groups which formed at the September 5 meeting reemerged. A group opposed to the dissent not only held out against acceptance of the Inquiry Report but also voted against the Trustees' recognition that the proposed conditions of silence (which never in fact were efficacious within the University community) were "no longer applicable" given the conclusion of the Inquiry. Thus, these Trustees continued to assert that the expression of dissent from *Humanae Vitae* should be banned at the University, as a permanent matter, and showed their fundamental concern not with the question of "manner and mode" but with the question of the right to dissent that was expressed in the Statement. A group of outright supporters of the academic freedom of the dissenting theologians fought the rejection of the Inquiry Report. But the question of acceptance of the Inquiry Report did not come to a vote. A third or "mediating" group of Trustees, which had backed the Inquiry plus suspension-or-silence arrangement, was disturbed by the Inquiry Report's severe criticism of the Trustees' September 5 arrangement, in particular, their invocation of the threat of suspension.

The Trustees voted unanimously to "receive" the Report for study, evaluation and response, and noted pointedly that the Report "was seven months in preparation but was submitted to the Board [of Trustees] only one week ago" (i.e., April 6). (The Report had in fact been submitted April 1 and mailed April 2, and the Trustees, through their representative in the Inquiry, had been privy to the entire hearing procedure and documentation. Also, the Chairman of the Inquiry Board was available at the Trustees' meeting, with the full record of the Inquiry, to answer any Trustee's questions about the Report.)

The Trustees thanked the participants on the Inquiry Board and the two Acting Rectors who had served during the Inquiry proceedings and reiterated their gratitude (first expressed in their December 23 letter) for the dissenting professors' observance of the Trustees' conditions of silence as set down on September 5:

> The Board of Trustees of The Catholic University of America should and hereby does express its gratitude for the cooperation of the members of the academic community for having abstained "for the period of the inquiry from any activities which would involve the name of the Catholic University and which are inconsistent with the pronouncements of the ordinary teaching authority established in the Church—above all, that of the Holy Father."

The Trustees asserted that "the conditions requested and *accepted* by the teachers involved are *no longer operative*" (emphasis supplied). As noted in previous chapters and particularly as confirmed by the Report of Committee A of the Academic Senate, which had been forwarded to the Trustees, the professors had never accepted the Trustees' conditions. Moreover, Committee A had also concluded that the only operative condition of silence was the AAUP ban on Inquiry publicity and, by letter of January 16, 1969, counsel for the subject professors advised the Trustees (through the Acting Rector) that they had rejected the requested conditions.

The Trustees also emphasized their concern with the *classroom* teaching of sacred science and the underlying substantive theological issues, as opposed to the "academic propriety" or "manner and mode" issue:

BE IT NOW RESOLVED: That the Board of Trustees of The Catholic University of America should and hereby does express its confidence that teachers of theology and other sacred sciences will carry out their teaching function and conduct their scholarly research consonant with their Roman Catholic faith commitment.

AND BE IT FURTHER RESOLVED: That the Board of Trustees of The Catholic University of America should and does hereby note that in accord with the usual academic practice and the Statutes of the University, the Faculty in its teaching of doctrine continues to be subject to the teaching authority of the Church, with specific recognition of the supreme teaching authority of the Holy See.

Finally, the Board of Trustees directed the Chairman of the Board to appoint a five-member committee to examine the Inquiry Report and report back to the Board of Trustees.

The Trustees, in conjunction with the release of the Inquiry Report at the conclusion of their Houston meeting, issued a press release which purported to describe the resolutions they had adopted and which named the members of the committee to review the Inquiry Report. This press release was materially inaccurate insofar as it omitted all reference to the doctrinal concern emphasized in the resolutions and altered the description of the resolution which had stated that the Trustees' condition of theological silence had been accepted to make it appear to refer to the AAUP condition of silence about the acts of the Inquiry.

After the meeting, the Chairman of the Board of Trustees remained in Houston and addressed the National Conference of Catholic Bishops, meeting there the week of April 14, in an appeal for funds for the University. Many of the bishops had fallen behind in their contributions to the university as assessed the previous year, and some had cited the dissent among the school theologians as the reason for their difficulty in meeting their quotas. For example, in a letter to the University dated February 24, 1969, Bishop William G. Connare, Bishop of Greensburg, Pennsylvania, had written:

. . . I, too, regret that the amount of our gift does not come anywhere near the suggested quota for the Diocese of Greensburg. It does, however, represent the gift of our people to the appeal in the name of the University. It further reflects the feeling of our priests and people toward the University at the time of the appeal last November. It will take a little time for the people to forget the earlier conduct of the School of Theology at the University. Many have said that they are waiting to see the eventual disposition of this problem.

I am delighted in the choice of Dr. Walton as President of the University, and I have so written to him. I see the need for Catholic University. I hope it can survive. I hope, too, that our priests and religious on the faculty and among the students will realize how much they have hurt the reputation of the University among the simple people, whose support to the annual appeal has been constant over the years. My prayers join those of all sincere friends of the University that the damage done a year ago can eventually be repaired in the minds of our people.

Similarly, in a letter to the University dated February 28, 1969, Bishop John L. Morkovsky, of the Galveston-Houston diocese (and a Trustee of the University), wrote:

. . . I am sure you are aware of the difficulty of presenting a good image of Catholic University to our most ·faithful people during this time of dissent by a number of its professors from the Holy Father's teaching. Although we are doing our best to tell our people that the present crisis is a passing moment in the life of the University, it is difficult to do this with great conviction or effectiveness.

The assessments for the dioceses in the country, however, had generally been doubled for the 1968–69 contributions as compared with the previous year's figures, so that what was purported to be a diminution was in some cases actually a net increase over the previous years' contributions.

There was, among the Bishops' letters concerning their financial support for the University, a most pointed attempt to exercise financial pressure in the disposition of the dissenters' case. Francis Cardinal McIntyre of Los Angeles, who had moved for the dissenters' "resignation" on September 5, wrote in a letter to the University dated February 28, 1969:

. . . We have made a nominal payment this year of $20,000. I shall be content with that payment until the matter of the revolting faculty of the University be settled. I shall make no further payment while the present impossible situation exists.

(In contrast, Cardinal O'Boyle, notwithstanding his impassioned opposition to the theological dissent from the Encyclical, has vigorously supported the University's finances and has urged his fellow bishops to do likewise.)

In the context of such financial pressure, the Chairman of the Board of Trustees addressed the bishops and discussed the needs of the University. As part of his presentation, the Chairman read to the bishops the resolutions adopted at the Trustees' Houston meeting which, among other things, contained the false statement that the dissenting professors had, at least during the Inquiry, accepted the condition of silence proposed by the Trustees. The Chairman also informed the bishops of the five-man committee of Trustees appointed to review the Inquiry Report.

The professors' counsel wrote to Cardinal Krol asking for copies of the resolution which the Trustees had adopted in Houston, offering their assistance to his work in reviewing the Inquiry Report, and requesting that under the norms of AAUP governing Trustee review of faculty reports in cases involving faculty discipline, they be informed if the "Krol Committee" began to consider actions against the professors inconsistent with the recommendations of the Inquiry Report. The Secretary of the Board of Trustees, on April 18, 1968, forwarded to the professors' counsel a copy of the resolutions adopted by the Board in Houston. Counsel for the University Trustees replied to the professors' counsel, on behalf of the Trustees, that no action would be taken by the Trustees until after the Krol Committee had reported.

After the Report of the Inquiry Board was made public, it was generally reported in the press that the professors had been vindicated by the findings of the Inquiry Board. The professors themselves publicly emphasized that the Report had not only favored the manner and mode of their dissent but also made the judgment that their theological dissent was a tenable theological position for Roman Catholics. The publicity surrounding the Inquiry Report focused new attention on the situation of the priests in the Archdiocese of Washington whose faculties had been suspended in varying degrees by Archbishop O'Boyle because they stated they would respect as a tenable Catholic position the responsible decision on the part of Roman Catholic spouses to use artificial contraception. Certain of the dissenting professors pointed out that the decision of the Inquiry Report, together with the actions of other bishops' conferences and theologians throughout the world, impeached the justice of the Washington situation. In addition, other published reports spoke of the far-reaching effects of the Inquiry Report on Catholic education and pastoral practice.

The attention of the Academic Senate was called to these various published interpretations of the Inquiry Report during the time in which the Trustees were studying the Report. A resolution was introduced at the June 4 meeting of the Academic Senate which specifically deplored a newspaper quotation in which one of the dissenters declared that the Report "completely vindicates our actions and declarations." Despite the fact that some of the Senators pointed out immediately that the foregoing quotation in its context within the news article in question obviously referred to the actions and declarations which had been the subject of the Inquiry, (i.e., the dissent from *Humanae Vitae*) the Senate returned to this subject at its meeting the next day and passed a resolution which began with a reference to "some misinterpretations of its action in accepting and approving the Board of Inquiry Report which implied that the Report supports all of the actions and declarations of the dissenting professors." That reference was neither specified in the resolution nor explained in the minutes of that meeting. The June 5 resolution of the Academic Senate went on to state:

> Because it is not within its competence, the Academic Senate was not approving or rejecting a particular theological position nor was it intending to pass judgment, directly or indirectly, on any action taken by any Ordinary in regard to the priests of his diocese.

But the resolution did not explain how the Senate could interpret its own prior conclusion that "the statement [of dissent] expresses a tenable theological position," does not constitute "approving . . . a particular theological opinion," since the theological tenability of a theological position is a theological opinion (and, in the birth control controversy, a crucial one). The Senate made no public press release of this resolution but voted that the resolution be transmitted to the Board of Trustees.

When the Trustees met again (in Washington, D.C.) on June 15 to consider the Krol Report, a six-page document was produced by Cardinal Krol. (Various committees of the Trustees had met during the day of June 14; it is not known whether the Krol Committee met then or then examined the 3,000-page record of the Inquiry. They had not met as of a week before the June Trustees' meeting.) The Trustees, through their Chairman, ordered the three faculty representatives (who are entitled to participate in all discussions of the Board of Trustees affecting the faculty) to leave the room for almost two hours while the Trustees considered the Krol report. Just before the Trustees recessed for lunch, the faculty representatives were readmitted and given copies of the Krol report to read during mealtime.

When the Trustees resumed their meeting after lunch, all copies of the Krol report given to faculty representatives were confiscated. A draft statement was then prepared by Cardinal Krol and others for release to the public. That press release accepted the report of the Faculty Board of Inquiry "insofar as it pertains to the academic propriety of the conduct of these faculty members [who had dissented from the Encyclical]." However, the Trustees purported to qualify their acceptance of the Inquiry Report. The Trustees asserted that they had directed an Inquiry "into the style, manner and mode of the dissent" of the professors and purported that acceptance of the Inquiry Report did not "represent approval of the theological position expressed" [by the dissenters]. In this connection, the Trustees did not mention their September 5 directive that the Inquiry consider the "declarations" as well as actions of the subject professors in the light of the Pontifical Statutes of the University, nor the December 23 letter which had specifically requested the Inquiry Board to consider the responsibility of the professors' conduct in the light of their Profession of Faith, as well as accepted academic norms; nor did they advert to the fact that Bishop Shannon, as the Trustees' representative in the Inquiry, had approved the Inquiry Board's view that it would have to pass on the theological tenability of the dissent in the light of the Trustees' September 5 mandate.

The Trustees, in attempting to qualify their acceptance of the Inquiry Report, did not acknowledge the Inquiry Board's and Academic Senate's censure of their threat to suspend the dissenting professors. In this connection, the Trustees also stated in their press release that their acceptance of the Inquiry Report "does not imply complete agreement that all findings are supported in the record."

After the meeting had concluded and the Statement accepting the Inquiry Report had been released, one of the hierarchical Trustees revealed to the Catholic press that there were "serious questions" about the theological position of the dissenters. It was also disseminated through the National Catholic News Service and widely reported in the Catholic press that the Trustees had voted to "support the Chancellor" in his decision to refer these questions, concerning the orthodoxy of the professors' dissent, to an extrinsic tribunal, namely, a commission of bishops under the auspices of the National Conference of Catholic Bishops.[1] The Trustees did not refer to the Chancellor's further inquiry into the dissent in their press statement which acknowledged acceptance of the Inquiry Report. They did report in that press release that their acceptance of the Report did not "represent approval of the theological position" of the dissenters, welcoming the "distinction" made by the University Academic Senate resolution of June 5. But the Inquiry Report approved by both the Senate and the Trustees made no distinction between "acceptance" of the Inquiry Report as to the "academic propriety" of the dissent and "approval" of the theological tenability of the dissent. Indeed, the Inquiry Report had affirmed that, with respect to the expressions of Roman Catholic theologians, "academic propriety" *requires* theological tenability within the field of the Catholic faith commitment. The Report also made clear that the recognition of academic freedom most assuredly does not imply University *approval or disapproval* of the opinions expressed in the exercise of that right.

Thus the fact that the Trustees would support the right of a fellow Trustee to continue to question the orthodoxy of the theologians' dissent does not in any way impeach the conclusion of the Inquiry Report (accepted by the Trustees) that the University itself could not continue to question that the "declarations and actions of the subject professors with respect to the Encyclical *Humanae Vitae,*" . . . "did not violate any of their obligations to Catholic University of America, did not offend against responsible academic procedure [and] did not depart from the spirit of the University."

Notes

1. National Catholic News Service (Domestic), June 17, 1969.

13

Reflections,
Analyses and Comments

In the preceding chapters we have set forth what we believe to be a fair report of the facts and all the extrinsic normative materials we presented to the Inquiry Board. As lawyers we live outside the university world and outside the ecclesiastical world, but at the same time it is our profession to deal with facts, with disputes and with norms; it is also our profession to seek the significance of facts in terms of the contextually controllable norms and to give advice for the future to the extent we foresee normative developments and can relate them to proposed courses of conduct. Hence we take the liberty of addressing to educators, churchmen and others who may be concerned our conclusions as to the significance of the facts of the Catholic University "birth control" controversy, as to the issues which were not resolved in the resolution of that controversy and as to what the future may hold or should hold for church-related schools and their sponsors. With less deference, we also offer certain recommendations in the area of academic freedom and due process generally.

The Significance of the Events

The functional significance of events in a society depends upon what its members know of the events and how they think of them. The most newsworthy of the events at Catholic University between July, 1968, and June, 1969, which are the subject of this book, were communicated to the public through the secular and the Catholic press—the Theologians' Statement of dissent, the

Chancellor's inquiry of August 20, the Trustees' mandate for a faculty inquiry, the threat to suspend the dissenters, the favorable Inquiry Report and the action of the Trustees in response to the Report. The treatment of the same events and of their significance by the secular press and a portion of the Catholic press on the one hand and by the remaining portion of the Catholic press (especially editorially) on the other hand was quite disparate. This phenomenon is a key to the significance of the events themselves.

In the secular press and certain portions of the Catholic press the theologians by their dissent were courageous, the Trustees' mandate for an inquiry was a giant step forward for Catholic University insofar as the dissenting theologians were to be accorded academic due process and not summarily dismissed, the Inquiry Report was a University action which vindicated the theologians and the principle of academic freedom and due process and the Trustees' ambiguous acceptance of the Report and expressed theological reservations were far less significant than the victory of the theologians in retaining their University status. In large portions of the Catholic press the theologians' dissent was treacherous, the Trustees' mandate for an inquiry during which the dissent was to be silenced was a first step in the required condemnation of the dissenters, the Inquiry Report was an intrusion of the profane secular world into the sacred religious world and the Trustees' purported nonacceptance of the theological tenability of the dissenters' position and authorization of further hierarchical proceedings properly rejected that intrusion and properly denied exoneration to the dissenters and their position.

Both versions of the events are equally correct and there is not any inconsistency between them. It is clear that the Trustees intended that two different versions of the affair be communicated to two different audiences. Those dual intentions, the Trustees' methods of implementing them and the knowledge and values they reveal are what we find most significant in the total experience.

From the very beginning of our representation of the subject professors, they have told us that, in their experiences at Catholic University, they have enjoyed a very large measure of academic freedom. To their knowledge, while there had been in the past several clear instances of denial of academic freedom in matters affecting institutionalized Roman Catholic positions, in the interval between the University reforms resulting from the "Curran affair" in the spring of 1967 and the "birth control" affair in the summer of 1968 there were no such instances and, indeed, the entire atmosphere at the University was growing more and more free and open. Also, notwithstanding the sharp criticisms we shall make of the Trustees' conduct in the "birth control" controversy, we call attention to the implicit assumptions of the Trustees (at least collectively) that they could not terminate the dissenting professors without a faculty hearing and that they could not reverse the final faculty judgment favorable to the professors. We note that faculty members from over 200 other Catholic educational institutions (mostly colleges and universities) also publicly subscribed to the Theologians' Statement of dissent and that none of the governing boards of those institutions took any adverse action in response. While we understand that certain of such governing boards were awaiting the outcome of the Catholic University proceedings, we seriously doubt that, if those proceedings had had an unfavorable outcome, any significant number of governing boards would have initiated proceedings against the dissenters on their faculties. Finally, we note our knowledge of two Catholic colleges or universities (Notre Dame and St. Peter's) at which the presidents defended the academic freedom of their dissenting theologians and of two members of the hierarchy (Cardinal Shehan in Baltimore and Archbishop Boland in Newark) who recognized the autonomy of the Catholic colleges and universities in their dioceses and discharged their legitimate ecclesiastical concerns by assuring themselves that what was taught as Roman Catholic theology would be Roman Catholic theology. Undoubtedly, there are many instances unknown to us of other university presidents and other bishops whose conduct in connection with faculty members' disset from the Encyclical reflected similar knowledge and similar values.

Hence, we recognize the enormous progress made toward the

autonomy of American Catholic colleges and universities (autonomy as human institutions of higher learning with their own values and their own structures) and toward full academic freedom at those institutions including freedom in controversial matters affecting their sponsoring church in its institutional form. We also recognize the legitimacy of the concerns of churchmen that colleges and universities which their church may sponsor should be of positive benefit to the church and should not perpetrate harm, from a religious point of view, on their students or on the church's communicants. However, we cannot dismiss the events at Catholic University as a fortuitous aberration or simply an interesting example of a synthesis of two antitheses (faith versus reason, Catholic versus university). The Catholic University events involved too many representative people to be irrelevant and, if ultimate antitheses were involved, the academic data or the Catholic data we presented in the preceding chapters are simply wrong. We see other significances in the events with which we were professionally concerned. Our views are based in part on our inferences from, and normative judgments of, the conduct to which we were exposed. Accordingly, we offer our views of what occurred.

The year of the Inquiry not only vindicated in part academic freedom and institutional autonomy at Catholic University and not only in part served the religious concerns of certain of the University's hierarchical sponsors, it also exposed the Board of Trustees' (treating it as an entity) mentality that it must "straddle" the concepts of "Catholic" and of "university," a use of rhetoric and a compromise of principle in place of candor and an implementation of principle, a functional lack of University autonomy vis-à-vis the hierarchy, ignorance of the futility of "adjudications" of intellectual issues and, sadly, duplicity, manipulations and falsifications by many ranking churchmen and University Trustees and administrators and the resulting corrosive moral effects of unconscionable compromise and unethical conduct.

Three days before the Theologians' Statement of dissent was promulgated, the Trustees of Catholic University had approved a Statement of Objectives which declared that the University was to function as a "free and autonomous center of learning." Those words were not borne out in the Trustees' actions of September 5.

The freedom and autonomy of universities depends ultimately on whether responsible officials show a true appreciation of the value of the principles which are the guarantors of such freedom and autonomy. Academic freedom is not simply another "interest" to be bartered and balanced with other competing and conflicting claims. Responsible officials of universities must not simply "respect" the principles of academic freedom to create an appearance of academic respectability, but rather must accept and apply them as the parameters of academic self-respect. The Trustees of Catholic University from the beginning of this Inquiry paid merely verbal respect for the principles of academic responsibility and fell short of a true understanding of these principles and failed at crucial times to act in accord with them. Indeed, the call for the Inquiry at Catholic University appeared to us not to be the exercise of responsible academic procedure but rather the use of the forms of due process to put a responsible dissent under a year-long cloud for the sake of the individual interests of certain of the Trustees of the University.

The record illustrates that after the Encyclical had been issued, the Vatican had instructed leaders of national hierarchies to suppress licit dissent from the Encyclical. Some members of the American hierarchy appear to have been particularly amenable to these instructions. It is equally evident that dominant members of the United States hierarchy, either because they acquiesced in those instructions, or because independently they reflected the mentality of the instructions, sought to accomplish such suppression at The Catholic University of America. They employed a combination of forces: legal powers as Trustees of the University corporation; financial powers as conduits through which funds donated by American Catholics to the University flow; and persuasive powers which inhere to the "superior to inferior" psychological relationship presently predominating between cardinals and bishops, bishops and priests and the hierarchy and laymen. Perhaps principally because of the hierarchy's use of financial pressure, the Administration of the University by and large cooperated with, or was at least passive in the face of, those efforts. In the process, the autonomy of the University became a myth.

Specific examples of the role of the Vatican in the Catholic University case include the letter of August 14, 1968, from its Secretary of State to the Chancellor of the University introduced at the September 5 Trustees' meeting and continued at least through delivery on April 1, 1969, of the then confidential report of the Board of Inquiry to the Apostolic Delegate, the Vatican's representative of the Church in the United States. The role of the American hierarchy, as such, in the Catholic University case began with the meeting on August 18-19, 1968, in New York among theologians (including representatives of the dissenting Catholic University professors) and representatives of the hierarchy. The legitimate purpose of the meeting was theological-pastoral dialogue—an informal, free and frank exchange of views. The one-sided account of the meeting laid before the University Trustees at their decisive meeting on September 5, 1968, however, was not only a perversion of the concept of dialogue but was a reflection of the inability of the hierarchy and the Trustees to distinguish the relationship between priest and bishop from the relationship between university teacher and university governing board. Indeed, Reverend Doctor Friedman testified as to this unspoken but unwarranted assumption during the Inquiry: that the hierarchy (as Trustees) must either endorse or negate the expressions of faculty members at "their" University

Other aspects of undue ecclesiastical influence include the oath of "silence" about the Vatican letter exacted from those present at the September 5 Board meeting (an attempt to create an obligation of untruthfulness about University affairs), which seems to be an ecclesiastical survival from inquisitorial precedents and was definitely inconsistent with fiduciary responsibility to the University community. The drafting instructions for the press release provided that the professors would be permitted to continue to teach only if they agreed to "desist from *criticism* of" the Encyclical, a hierarchical objective and, under any educational analysis (Catholic or secular), not a proper university objective. Indeed, those instructions were even broadened in the final form of the press release, which forbade (pending the Inquiry) faculty expressions inconsistent with any pronouncement of the Pope or the rest of the Church's hierarchical teaching authority. Finally, the press release was promptly mailed by the University administration to all the bishops of the United States (but not to the subject professors).

The need for the University to placate the American hierarchy and the relationship of the Trustees' silence-or-suspension threat against the dissenting professors to hierarchical positions was made evident by the Acting Rector's report of September 18, 1968, to "The Bishops of the United States" (not the Trustees of the University) which falsely stated that the dissenting professors had agreed to the conditions for continued teaching, i.e., the condition of silence outlined by the Trustees. This false report was reiterated in the Trustees' letter of December 23, 1968, to the Faculty Inquiry Board. Finally, after the professors had again informed the Trustees that they had not agreed to silence (and, indeed, had continued to publish their dissent), the Trustees again, in their resolutions of April 13, 1969, deferring consideration of the Inquiry Report, referred to the conditions "accepted" by the professors. This latter inference was included in the official minutes of the meetings and was read to the American bishops, but it was not included in the press release accompanying the announcement that the Trustees had sent the Inquiry Report to committee.

The suspension-or-silence arrangement underscored the *hierarchical* purposes involved in the Trustees' call for the Inquiry. Indeed, it seems to us that no "university" interest justified either the form of Inquiry which the Trustees mandated or their accompanying attempt to silence the dissent. The Inquiry Report showed that there were *no* "serious questions" raised by the theologians' dissent in terms of their academic responsibilities. But that fact could and should have been clear to the Trustees on September

5, if they had themselves acted responsibly. Certainly there were questions raised about the theologians' conduct that are and will be the subject of continuing religious debate. Some asked and continue to ask whether the substance of the professors' dissent is tenable in Catholic theology and whether the "manner and mode" of promulgating their dissent is a permissible method for Catholic theologians. The Transcript of the Chancellor's meeting of August 20 and a full account of the Statler-Hilton meeting of August 18-19, in the context of other dissenting declarations and actions of respected theologians and bishops throughout the world, however, should have convinced reasonable men that there clearly were existing differences of opinion within the Church on these questions. The Trustees evidently failed to give attention to the Transcript of the Chancellor's meeting (which was available to them on September 5); they heard only one side's report on the Statler-Hilton meeting. Had the Trustees properly informed themselves of the existing situation, they perhaps would have realized that the Inquiry which they mandated was an inappropriate forum for resolving the existing differences within the Catholic Church.

Any "inquiry" which requires a judgment concerning the *responsibility* of particular individuals has an essentially accusatorial nature. Legal history shows that such judicial fora are poor instruments for determining the ultimate rightness or wrongness of intellectual positions. While the Crown's forces may have to some degree suppressed religious dissent in seventeenth century England, the "state" trials held under one pretext or another never resolved the religious-intellectual controversies then raging. Similarly, the Galileo and Scopes trials never resolved the issues they purported to adjudicate; the loyalty proceedings conducted in many fora in the United States in the 1950's did not resolve the question of what is loyalty to one's country; and the very recent trials originating in issues raised by the Vietnam war can never resolve those issues.

At times, indeed, the legitimate interest of a university in passing on the professional qualifications of its members requires that judgments be made as to whether certain declarations or actions are within a given pale of competency. In this particular case, however, the dissenters could have been found incompetent and hence irresponsible (as the Trustees queried) only if their declarations or actions were found to be "untenable" within the pale of Catholic theological activity. This was the only meaningful question posed by the Trustees to the Inquiry. But had the Trustees made even a preliminary effort to inform themselves of the existing theological state of affairs (such as reading the Transcript of the Chancellor's meeting) they would have seen that there could be no "serious question" as to the tenability of the theologians' dissent or their "manner and mode." The Trustees should have realized that the very fact of existing differences of views on these matters within the pale of Catholic theology precluded any question as to whether a declaration or action within that pale was irresponsible theologically.

Nor was there any reason to question the theologians' compliance with the *general* norms of responsibility in extramural expression applicable to all academicians. AAUP observers present at the Chancellor's meeting saw no violations of academic norms and specifically denied that the dissenters had misused the University's name in connection with their Statement.

Furthermore, the Trustees had no business to endorse publicly any complaints of "constituents" of the University with respect to the dissent of the professors until they had informed themselves of the proper criteria for judging those complaints. The Trustees later admitted (on December 23, 1968) their ignorance of whether norms of responsible academic procedure applicable to the subject conduct were even in existence; nevertheless, on September 5, they publicly asserted that the subject conduct "raised serious questions" with respect to "responsible academic procedure." If the Trustees were indeed unaware of the *existence* of norms of responsible academic procedure, how could they judge that the "questions" concerning academic procedure they heard were "serious" enough to warrant an immediate inquiry into the personal responsibility of the subject professors? Moreover, as the Inquiry Report shows, if they *were* aware of the existing norms of responsible academic procedure, how could they view the questions they heard as "serious"? It appears most likely that the Trustees were, in fact, ignorant of existing norms of academic responsibility. Indeed, implicit in the Trustees' call for an Inquiry was the suggestion that special religious limitations might be applicable to extramural academic expression, a proposition refuted by the plain meaning of the basic 1940 Statement of AAUP.

The Trustees also took their September 5 action at least in part in the context of serious misstatements of fact. The Chancellor recited to the Trustees nonexistent press quotations making two of the dissenters appear to be irresponsible. While perhaps no Trustee could, at the meeting, immediately verify the accuracy of the Chancellor's fabricated press quotations, merely reading the Transcript of the August 20 meeting would have required a challenge of the Chancellor's patent misstatement to the September 5 meeting of the Board that the professors were unable to furnish any support to their right to dissent. Nor does the record show that the Chancellor was asked why he had unilaterally breached his agreement with the dissenters to give them until October 1 to present appropriate written materials and had instead called for the special Trustees' meeting on September 5. Those who are responsible for misstatements of fact must bear the chief responsibility, but the Trustees nonetheless put themselves in the position of acting publicly, at least in part, on the basis of misinformation. In addition, the Trustees made no effort even to defer the question of the dissent; they later put off action on the Inquiry Report for two months. They made no effort to hear the dissenters' side of the issues.

Why would persons otherwise reputed to be responsible unanimously commit themselves, at a hasty, one-day meeting, to such an irresponsible course of action? The record shows an explanation: on September 5, the Trustees were prepared to take direction from the Vatican and from hierarchical financial sponsors of the University. They recognized the dangers of censure of the University that might result from the precipitous firing of the dissenters, which some of the hierarchical sponsors of the University (e.g., Cardinal McIntyre) desired. Such action would have brought distinct embarrassment to the University as an academic institution. Many Trustees obviously sought to mollify those members of the Board who demanded action against the dissenters. They raised questions about the professors' dissent which they said were "serious" enough to justify a University Inquiry into that dissent. The pendency of the Inquiry, in turn, can be seen as an attempt to give a color of procedural respectability to the effort to obtain an interim silencing of the dissent by means of a threat of suspension. They made a show of mere "respect" for the accepted procedural norms by purporting that they were invoking the suspension arrangement "in accord with" the relevant AAUP standards. The Trustees may well have settled on the Inquiry and suspension format expecting that their mere reference to the principle of a hearing and the norms of AAUP would satisfy their duties to the University community.

Once it became evident that the Trustees were not going to make any charges to back up the "serious questions" they spoke of on September 5, however, their threat of suspension lost any color of procedural justification under the norms of AAUP. The Trustees attempted to rationalize, in the December 23 letter to the Inquiry Board, their purpose in threatening to suspend the dissenting professors: "The Board endeavored to create a climate within which the current review could be conducted with charity, clarity and out of the heat of controversy." The suggestion that the purpose of the Trustees' suspension threat was "charitable" is a patronizing hypocrisy. The threat of suspension was never enforced, in any case, but the University administration had purported to the bishops that the threat had been efficacious, and was thus able to create the false impression in the minds of its chief financial sponsors that an interim silencing of dissent had been achieved.

The Inquiry itself also proved to be useful to the hierarchical sponsors of the University. The Inquiry put the dissenters under a professional cloud, discrediting them within the Church and making them prove the innocence of their dissent. The inquiry which the Trustees called for was to be no mere "fact finding" process or even a grand jury style hearing to determine whether wrongdoing was to be charged. The Trustees asked the Inquiry to determine whether the subject professors had "violated their responsibilities," not merely whether there was "probable cause to charge them with violating their responsibilities." The time-consuming burden of the Inquiry also served to divert the professors from their normal professional activities and prevented them from answering many of the scurrilous charges made against them in certain publications during the pendency of the proceedings. Moreover, in view of the seriousness of the Inquiry mandated by the Trustees, the dissenting professors were constrained to clear with us, as legal counsel, before making any public statements during the Inquiry.

The Trustees, in effect, put upon the professors an ultimate burden of defending themselves against a "guilty" verdict. Surely in this instance the process had become "accusatory" rather than merely "investigatory," and all the professors' procedural rights should have come into play. But, as noted, the Trustees would not come forward with any specific charges of wrongdoing, and, indeed, denied that they meant to make any accusations against the dissenters. The dissenting professors were given the "due process" right of a faculty hearing. The University had learned that lesson of due process during the "Curran affair" two years earlier. But due process is only a *means* to academic freedom and there is little academic freedom where the price of its exercise is a year spent under an unjustified professional cloud.

The same pressures which moved the Trustees to misuse the vehicles of academic due process also produced on the University's administrative officials certain other moral effects during the course of the Inquiry. One example was the conduct of the Acting Rector in making a false report to the United States bishops on September 18, 1968, and the failure of the subsequent Acting Rector to correct the falsehood when specifically directed to do so by the Academic Senate resolution accepting the Report of its Committee A on March 6, 1969, or when the falsehood was reiterated for the benefit of the bishops in the Trustees' second resolution of April 13, 1969. These moral effects are also reflected by the conduct of the President-elect of the University when, without any reliable knowledge whatsoever of the faculty recruitment procedures of the University's School of Theology or the academic careers of the subject professors, affirmed in a press interview (during the pendency of the Inquiry) with a reporter for a Catholic diocesan newspaper that the faculty of that School should not be built on teachers who had "worn out their welcome" at local seminaries.[1] That same President-elect helped to draft the Trustees' final press release of June 16, 1969, which failed to reveal the Trustees' vote of support for a continuing inquiry into the dissenters' orthodoxy.

The nakedness of the hierarchical use of financial coercion, even in violation of a double trusteeship (that for the benefit of the University and that for the benefit of those from whom contributions were received for transmittal to the University) was illustrated by Cardinal McIntyre's letter of February 28, 1969, bluntly announcing that he was withholding funds "until the matter of the revolting faculty of the University be settled."

American hierarchical pronouncements had a direct impact on the course of the Inquiry proceeding. Prior to publication of the November, 1968, Pastoral Letter of the United States bishops recognizing the right of a *theologian* to scholarly dissent from the Encyclical (even publicly in some cases) the Acting Rector, on behalf of the Trustees, had told the subject professors they would be spared the Inquiry if they recanted their dissent. Following that 1968 Pastoral Letter, the Trustees, in the letter of December 23, 1968, advised the Inquiry Board that "at no time in this inquiry is there any attempt by the Board [or Trustees] to question the right of a scholar to have or to hold private dissent on Papal teaching not defined as infallible."

The December 23 letter on behalf of the Trustees was patently dishonest. It was specifically dishonest in pretending that the September 5 action of the Trustees did not charge that the Theologians' Statement was beyond the pale of legitimate Roman Catholic theology. It was implicitly dishonest when it suggested that the Trustees' purpose was to initiate some sort of study commission of norms of responsibility (as distinguished from accusatorial proceedings against 20 individuals who were to be silenced during its pendency). It was foolishly dishonest when it said that the Trustees were unaware of the existence of norms of academic freedom in matters of public academic debate.

Even as the Trustees ultimately accepted portions of the Inquiry Report, their service of the hierarchy's interests continued. In response to the September 5 mandate of the Trustees and their specific question (in the December 23 letter) whether the professors had violated their "profession of faith," the Inquiry Board had passed on the theological "tenability" (in "Roman Catholic theology") of the dissenting "declaration" itself. The Trustees, nevertheless, tried to distinguish their acceptance of the Report from accepting the Report's functional theological judgment that the substance of the dissent was, indeed, "tenable." But that attempt was itself most revealing, since it showed definitely that the real issue, for the Trustees, was fundamentally the "orthodoxy" of the dissent, not the "manner and mode" or "timing" or "quickness" of the dissent. The Trustees, after accepting the Inquiry Report, declared their own support for the University Chancellor's challenge to the orthodoxy of the dissenters' position, which challenge he proposed to lay before the National Conference of Catholic Bishops. These developments occurred despite the fact that the Inquiry Report which the Trustees accepted as to its academic propriety conclusions had found that academic propriety required that the dissent be tenable in Catholic theology and had concluded that no further proceedings questioning the subject professors' fitness to teach because of their dissent should be instituted. Thus the Trustees ended the year of Inquiry in compromise, as they had begun it. Instead of wholehearted acceptance of the Inquiry Report and the principles of university autonomy and academic freedom which it articulated, it appears to us that the Trustees again chose to mollify those among their number who disagreed with the dissent, clearly not a legitimate university objective.

It seems clear to us that the *use* of Catholic University, in an attempt to discredit the professors by putting them under such unwarranted inquiries was the product of the University's lack of functional autonomy from its sponsoring body. This subjugation was enforced, with the help of those too ready to sell the principle of autonomy, by the University's hierarchical Trustees.

The foregoing phenomena are symptomatic of serious problems and impending crises. We refer to problems of knowledge and values. Many governing board members and administrators of Catholic colleges and universities and many members of the American hierarchy are woefully deficient in their knowledge of academic freedom and due process. Some simply reject university autonomy as a positive value and many accept it with the reservation that it be inapplicable where direct institutional interests of the Church are concerned. Many assume that religious harm flows from any spill-over from the academic world to the parish world of the intellectual controversies in the Church or of the painful tensions produced by attempts to distinguish religion from culture and resistance to those attempts. Many reject the notion that, if the price to be paid for protecting their uneducated communicants is to make the schools they sponsor irrelevant to their students, at that time in the future when virtually all are educated, their churches may be empty. And many, notwithstanding their high calling, succumb to the constant human temptation to employ immoral means to achieve what they conceive to be a good or useful result.

It can be said that the Trustees of Catholic University and its administrators acted thus only to avert a crisis which may have destroyed the University. Firing the subject professors would have destroyed the University academically; failing to take action against them could have destroyed the University financially. Esoteric morality aside, the Trustees' conduct proved justified because they evidently succeeded. A governing board must be pragmatic and live in the "real" world. Perhaps matters of principle were compromised and perhaps the tactics employed were questionable, but no visible damage has resulted. Indeed, on balance the result was a victory for the dissenting professors—they remain free to teach at the University and their hierarchical attackers have been frustrated; while some injustice may have been visited on twenty men, that is a small price to pay to save the University, and no battle can be fought without casualties. With all this we are in serious disagreement. Accepting the basic "idea of a university," if truth and principle are no longer to exist what has been saved? Even from a pragmatic point of view, it is not clear that the University has been saved.

The apparent success of this "realism" and "pragmatism" may create the belief that future crises can be similarly resolved. Assuming continuation of present trends in university life and in church life, we seriously doubt that a future crisis of the magnitude of the *Humanae Vitae* crisis (or even one of lesser magnitude) can be resolved by pragmatism. Perhaps the next time threatened professors will say, "we will not teach subject even to an appearance of extraneous conditions laid down by trustees"; or students will say, "we will not attend classes if teachers are threatened with extraneous restraints on their teaching"; or faculties will say, "we will not lend academic respectability to unwarranted and suppressive academic proceedings." Perhaps too many financial supporters will say, "we will not support a university whose faculty opposes our ecclesiastical views"; or theologians will say, "we will not accept employment at a nonautonomous university"; or students will say, "we will not enroll in such a university." As with other ambivalent institutions in our society, the days of the church-related school which attempts a "straddle" of basic issues are numbered.

Some Suggested Remedies

It is easy to articulate generalized remedies for the problems which inhere in the present situation: education about academic freedom and due process and their inescapable necessity at a university, education about the consistency between faith and an autonomous university and between pastoral concerns and the endeavors of an autonomous university and, most importantly, an "open book" style of administration in which nothing is done or said which cannot be disclosed to the world freely and without embarrassment. Drawing on our experiences both in professional life generally and in the Inquiry proceedings in particular, we offer certain specific remedies.

The basic problem of the conflict of interest which inheres in a trustee of a Church-sponsored university who is a Church official must be faced. In our complex society, in which a single individual often has a plurality of functions with divergent responsibilities, we have developed considerable experience with problems of conflicts of interest. Since university trustees are typically chosen from a broad spectrum of university constituencies, including financial supporters and, in the case of Church-related schools, high-ranking churchmen, it is inevitable that various potential conflicts of interests will inhere in most trustees. A similar problem exists in modern American corporate life where, however, the problem is made manageable by an acute awareness of its existence.

Nor is the problem of conflicts of interest in trustees unique to Church-related schools. A corporate president on a university board of trustees probably will not be instinctively objective when dealing with university situations with a strong antibusiness impact, nor a retired admiral or general when the impact is antimilitary, nor a trustee of any background with strong political views when the impact is adverse to those views. However, awareness of one's conditioned inclinations coupled with deliberation and an experience in functioning objectively permits a person largely, if not perfectly, to achieve a reasonably objective position in a controversial matter consistent with the fiduciary role he is then fulfilling.

Needless to say, not every member of a university governing board will be an expert in, or passionately devoted to, the principles of academic freedom, but he must at least consciously and deliberately accept academic freedom as a university value of which he is a fiduciary. As a next step he must recognize that he is not an expert in the meaning of academic freedom and the subtleties of its implementation. Again, lack of specific expertise is a phenomenon with corporate director-fiduciaries insofar as they, like university trustees, deal with many problems that are beyond their respective orientations, skills and experiences. Corporate fiduciaries, nevertheless, are capable of functioning effectively when they are prepared to listen and learn from experts in particular fields and to make decisions only after having studied the data prepared by experts and only after having taken into account and given due weight to judgments and opinions of experts. University boards of trustees are certainly capable of functioning in the same way and undoubtedly many do so.

Thus, it seems clear that it should not be impossible for a member of the hierarchy to be a good university trustee even in the context of controversies which deeply involve his church's ecclesiastical positions. Existing AAUP norms (the special limitations" clause of Paragraph (b) of the 1940 Statement) suggest one way in which legitimate interests of Church-sponsors may be preserved without violating the academic integrity and autonomy of the university concerned. However, we think that a better approach was suggested on the course of the Inquiry proceedings. There is no need for special limitations on academic freedom in church-related schools, even in the classroom, if the criterion of professional competency is properly understood and applied, by academic peers, in respect of teachers of church-related subject matter. Within the Catholic context, the judgment by peers (which is to be the juridically effective judgment for academic purposes) must, of course, give due weight to the pronouncement of the Church's hierarchical magisterium. In this way the authority of the magisterium and the autonomy of the university are both preserved.

If one assumes, as has so often been postulated, that there is no true conflict between the good of religion and the good of society, between theological scholarship and truth and science and between American university values and religious values, a properly dedicated and properly disposed churchman who is willing to listen and learn should be able to function as a good university trustee. However, to do so he must be willing to suffer criticism and even a certain amount of rejection on the part of his fellow churchmen who may be less dedicated and less well disposed to, if not specifically ignorant of, the values and subtleties of academic freedom. It is a safe assumption that corporate executives suffer similar modest penalties in the business community in which they live when, in their role as university trustees, they take a stand which is misunderstood by or offensive to the business communities. If a person is unwilling to be faithful to his educational trust in the face of external pressures on his life and career, he should not be a university trustee.

Lay trustees of Church-related schools should not assume that their proper role is to defer to churchmen on the board even when the issue involved has religious implications, and churchmen trustees should treat lay trustees as equals in respect of all their common concerns about the university. It is unfortunate that the mystique of churchmen, particularly members of the hierarchy, may produce virtually a lay abstention in matters of university controversies with religious implications.

Surely church-related institutions of higher learning are valuable to our society, enriching it from the point of view of human values (in the highest sense of the word "human"). But unless governing boards of such institutions function on the basis that academic freedom, properly understood, is a primary university goal, not incompatible with religion,· unless trustees of Church-related universities function as fiduciaries for the university and unless laymen and churchmen are equally respected and equally active as university trustees, then there is serious doubt that Church-related universities will survive. If they cannot survive, our society will have only secular universities and sectarian propaganda institutes, and the ultimate goal of the churchman will be defeated. A sectarian propaganda institute is not a university, and qualified students and faculty members who seek "university" life will not be available to it.

These conclusions are equally applicable to those aspects of university life which involve theological scholarship. Until recent times, theological scholarship in the United States was largely denominational, and a scholar of a particular confessional commitment had to pursue his scholarship within the institutional educational framework sponsored by his church. Those conditions were first removed in non-Catholic institutions (consider, for example, Union Theological Seminary in New York), and it is a fact of American Catholic life that those limitations on Catholic theological scholarship are now disappearing. A Catholic theologian can now pursue his scholarship and his teaching in a non-Catholic institution (and typically at higher salary scales and with more attractive arrangements for research assistance, sabbaticals and the like). Thus, limiting Catholic theology schools to a para-orthodox theology will not solve any problem. While older Catholic scholars may not be very mobile, the younger ones surely are, and there is much evidence that they are seeking careers outside the unduly restrictive atmosphere of certain Catholic colleges and universities. Hence, making the Catholic University theologians unacceptable within what should be their natural milieu will neither silence them, diminish their prestige nor thwart their scholarly progress. Their voices will continue to be heard throughout the world, including the Catholic world. Should this trend continue, the more able students will seek the better scholarly training available outside the Catholic institutional framework, and the Catholic Church will forfeit its institutionalized intellectual activities.

Administrators of Catholic colleges and universities must face their day of reckoning as well. All university administrators face staggering financial problems. Most university administrators must work very hard and utilize all their ingenuity to achieve even a partial solution of their institutions' financial problems. They must maintain good alumni relations and good foundation relations. They must oversee the organization of time-consuming and critical fund-raising campaigns. Many church-related schools have had the luxury of relying on their sponsoring churches to weather financial crises. The Catholic University of America relies heavily on annual financial contributions from the American bishops. This support indeed saves much work and worry for the University's administrators, but it can also produce a most abject financial dependence. This annual financial subsidy exacts a rather heavy price in terms of autonomy as a university.

Unless a sponsoring religious body is prepared to support a *university,* without being able to restrict its academic freedom, church-related institutions of higher learning must choose between full-fledged American university status, with its attendant financial problems, and something less than that status, with its attendant mitigation of financial problems. In making this choice, long and hard consideration should be given to the proposition advanced by Reverend Doctor Friedman in his expert testimony during the Inquiry: "A university can afford to be poor but not unfree."

Some Procedural Recommendations

Not all utilizations of the inquiry technique are abusive. In many cases it will be impossible for the faculty to determine at the outset whether the inquiry is legitimate. However, should it become clear during the course of an inquiry that its invocation was unjustifiable under AAUP standards, the faculty should not be without remedy. Inquiries that are merely fact-finding, without any *ad hominem* focus and without any normative implications must in this respect be distinguished from inquiries (such as the Catholic University Inquiry) which are obviously and by their own terms directed to the question of whether certain specified individuals have "violated their responsibilities." A governing board or an administration is entitled to faculty assistance in determining, in a confused situation, what actually happened on a factual level, and it is also entitled to faculty assistance in any true study project. However, where the accusatorial inquiry is itself an effective deterrent to academic freedom, it should not be tolerated.

As noted, the subject professors and their counsel devoted 10,000 hours and incurred expenditures of $8,000 in preparing and presenting their materials to the Inquiry Board. In contrast,

the Chancellor's August 20, 1968, meeting with the subject professors and other members of the University faculty, which should
have been the end of the matter at the University, lasted about
three hours, and those faculty members who incurred expenses
in attending the meeting were reimbursed by the University. The
professors' burdens and expenses in the Inquiry would have
been far smaller had the Trustees come forward with a bill of
particulars in respect of their charges of academic irresponsibility.
The Trustees were unable to do so, and the professors were faced
with the unfair choice of not participating in the Inquiry and
risking an unfavorable outcome, or of assuming the burden of
going forward affirmatively to justify, under all possible criteria,
all their declarations and actions with respect to the Encyclical
during the five-week period July 29-September 5, 1968. For good
and sufficient reason, the decision was to go forward and that
involved detailing the professional lives of 20 men over a five-
week period, organizing into a form comprehensible to educated
laymen extensive theological materials, researching and analyzing
an entire corpus of materials on academic freedom and academic
responsibility and obtaining expert witnesses from all over the
country and Canada to corroborate every aspect of the professors' case.

Some deterrent to this type of burden might be achieved if
AAUP procedural norms were modified to incorporate a provision that a faculty hearing panel be authorized to award to a
respondent who was exonerated his costs and expenses in the
proceedings. This is a traditional deterrent to unjustified litiga-
tion and, although the amounts involved may be too small to alter
the course of a university governing board, nevertheless the right
to reimbursement might mitigate to some extent the deterrent
effect of threats of burdensome inquiries on the exercise of academic
freedom.

University faculties must play a larger role in achieving academic freedom than simply supply able people to constitute faculty
hearing panels. In the case of faculty hearings mandated by
governing boards or administrations without probable cause under

AAUP standards, the faculty should refuse to conduct an inquiry or dismissal proceeding. While this might cause a temporary crisis, it would be an effective way of teaching those who would abuse AAUP processes to accomplish improper purposes that, so far as the faculty is concerned, they will not be able to do so and preserve any appearance of respectability. Finally, Catholic colleges and universities and certain other church-related schools face a unique problem in the area of academic freedom and due process. Most members of their faculties of theology and other sacred sciences are subject to ecclesiastical or religious superiors. Such a superior can "order" the faculty member to leave his teaching assignment and to take up another assignment for reasons which may be quite legitimate or which may be quite arbitrary or which may amount to a suppression of academic freedom. Putting aside the educational inefficiency involved, any reassignment prompted by a teacher's exercise of his academic freedom is morally contemptible and an abuse of authority (and, by forcing on the teacher an impossible conflict of conscience, incredibly cruel). The Inquiry Report suggested the possibility of protective contractual arrangements, presumably among the bishop or religious superior in question, the teacher and the educational institution. As lawyers we offer our view that a meaningful contract would be difficult to draft; furthermore, adjudications of claimed breaches of contract and efficacious remedies for adjudicated breaches may present insoluble problems.

It must be recognized that there may be legitimate reasons for the transfer of a cleric or religious teacher to another post, including a nonacademic post. It must also be recognized that it would be impossible to articulate in advance specific circumstances in which a proposed transfer would violate the academic freedom of a teacher. Hence, we can make no better suggestion than that the bishop or religious superior who permits one subject to his ecclesiastical jurisdiction to accept a university appointment formally pledge himself not to take any action which would violate the teacher's academic rights and that the university corporation formally pledge itself to the teacher that it will support him in the event of any such violation, including retention of him on the faculty notwithstanding any episcopal or religious disciplinary action.

In the Catholic University case, the perversion of process engaged in by the Trustees was not immediately known. As late as December 23, the Trustees insisted that in fact many persons inside the Church and others, including members of the general faculty of the University, had raised questions about the dissent which led them to call for the Inquiry. On January 10, 1969, however, the Trustees' representative could not name anyone specifically who had raised questions about the dissent, and stated that the Trustees had been influenced to make their decision by friends and by newspaper reports. By that time, however, the Inquiry proceedings were becoming in some measure an investigation of the Trustees' conduct as well as the professors' dissent.

The faculty of Catholic University, and, specifically the Inquiry Board, then, certainly cannot be faulted for going forward with the Inquiry given the slow discovery of the fact that the Trustees lacked any legitimate basis for their action of September 5.

However, the faculty "representatives" who attended the September 5 meeting unfortunately became implicated in the Trustees' action from the first. Indeed, Bishop Shannon testified during the Inquiry that they had "commended" the Trustees' suspension-or-silence arrangement. Whatever the truth of the matter, (*i.e.,* perhaps the representatives "commended" the Inquiry-plus-suspension merely as an alternative to summary dismissal) it was clear that the faculty representatives had been placed in a difficult position by the Trustees' inexplicable haste and particularly by the oath of silence that was the price of their full participation in the Trustees' meeting. When the Trustees met to consider the "Krol report" on the Inquiry, the faculty representatives were excluded. The experiment with faculty participation in Trustee decision-making at Catholic University thus has produced valuable lessons for all universities considering such arrangements. The primary lesson is that the faculty delegates must guard against being implicated in trustee compromises on matters of academic principle. Secondly, faculty delegates to a governing board, whatever their voting powers, must always be held to strict reporting requirements by the general faculty bodies, and trustees must be willing to admit faculty delegates to their meetings concerning faculty affairs with the understanding that no "oaths of secrecy" or other rubrics of confidentiality will be imposed to prevent the faculty delegates from reporting back to their own constituents in the faculty. Likewise, trustees must be willing to defer action respecting the faculty (such as the Inquiry and threat of suspension in this case) until the faculty representatives have an opportunity for meaningful consultation with their colleagues on the issues involved.

Another factor affecting the work burdens of professors subject to hearings is the composition of the faculty hearing panel. Ideally, a faculty panel should be composed of teachers whose field of competence is the academic field of the respondent professor. This would sharply reduce the work burdens of the proceedings on all concerned and tend toward a swifter and more just result. Nevertheless, the professors and their counsel in the Catholic University case sought a hearing panel broadly representative of the University because they believed that the response to the Trustees should be the response of the entire University faculty, not merely the Schools of Theology, Philosophy and Canon Law and the Department of Religious Education at which the dissenting professors taught. Collaterally, it appeared that it would be difficult to obtain a full panel of sacred sciences scholars who had not theretofore committed themselves on the issues involved. The composition of the faculty panel ultimately must be a function of the circumstances in question. When an issue of scholarly competence is involved, however, there should be a presumption in favor of a panel composed of scholars in the relevant field, and when an issue of personal misconduct is involved, scholars from the subject teacher's field should be represented on the faculty panel so that their expertise and the possible relationship of personal misconduct to fitness to teach in that field will be reflected in the ultimate result.

Another aspect of proceedings in respect of a faculty member to which attention should be given is the problem of prejudice to a nontenured teacher who is required to devote a significant portion of his probationary period to justifying challenged conduct in a burdensome proceeding. To the extent to which achieving tenure is a function of publication and classroom performance (itself a function of preparation), it is clear that a nontenured faculty member can be severely prejudiced by being subjected to an inquiry. This issue was raised with the Catholic University Vice-President for Academic Affairs, only to receive the response "they should have thought of that before they signed the Statement" [dissenting from the Encyclical]. Thus it seems that university administrations will not only at times be insensitive to this unfair prejudice but indeed may find it convenient. Accordingly, it might be suggested that the AAUP procedural standards be revised to provide also that no adverse administration action be taken with respect to a faculty member subjected to inquiry or dismissal proceedings and, to avoid inadvertent tenuring of teachers, that each academic term or each academic year (depending on the applicable tenure system) in which a faculty member is so subjected be added to the total maximum permissible probationary period (unless the University was prepared to grant tenure to him sooner).

Appropriate discovery procedures also would work to preclude the possibility that faculty members under inquiry will, like the Catholic University dissenters, bear the burden of proving their innocence. The October 16 Rules for the conduct of the Inquiry provided that the faculty board would assist the parties "in securing the attendance or written testimony of witnesses and the production of pertinent documentary evidence." When Bishop Shannon testified at the January 10 pre-Inquiry conference that at the Trustees' meeting on September 5 no person in an ecclesiastical position had demanded that action be taken "or any kind of memorandum like that," the professors and their counsel were unaware of the fact that a letter from the Vatican urging that action be taken against dissenters had been produced (subject to a secrecy oath) at the Trustees' September 5

meeting. Upon first learning of such a letter, the professors' counsel made a discovery request of the Inquiry Board pursuant to
the October 16 Rules. The Inquiry Board recognized the propriety of the request (there being no conceivable doubt that the
professors were entitled to make of record all the data on which
the Trustees based their actions on September 5 against the
subject professors). The University administration, however, would
not furnish a witness to testify as to the substantial accuracy and
completeness of the minutes of the September 5 meeting (which
made no mention of the Vatican letter). The Inquiry Board
Chairman was later to report that he understood that a matter
was discussed at the Trustees' meeting which was not recorded
in the minutes, but that he did not know what that matter was.
Thus the hearing tribunal, in the end, lacked *power* to obtain
relevant evidence to which the subject professors were entitled
under the rules applicable to the hearings. In a judicial proceeding
if a litigant should fail to produce data properly requested
by his adversary, the court has power to hold the refusing party
in contempt or to enter a favorable judgment to the party denied
access to the data, either on the issue in question or on the case
as a whole. (The choice among these remedies depends on the
circumstances.) This power is based on a fundamental premise
that a judicial proceeding is not a game of hide and seek, and that
fundamental fairness requires that a party be given access to
information in the possession of the other which is relevant to the
issues between them or which could lead to the discovery of
relevant information. It is difficult to think of any reason why a
university governing board should be entitled to initiate a proceeding against faculty members and then withhold relevant data
from the tribunal conducting the proceeding. It may not be
possible to vest in academic hearing tribunals the *power* to compel
the production of evidence. However, it seems feasible that AAUP
procedures could provide that when a university administration
fails to furnish data in its possession which the faculty hearing
panel determines to be properly requested (either by the tribunal

itself or by the subject professor), the proceedings should be terminated with prejudice to further proceedings against the professor in question on the charges made. The denial of access to pertinent data proved not to be prejudicial in the Catholic University case in light of the favorable result of the Inquiry. Had the Inquiry result been unfavorable, however, in light of present knowledge as to the nature of the concealed document and discussion at the Trustees' meeting on September 5, the inability of the Inquiry Board to obtain this information could very well have been critical and resulted in fundamental unfairness to the subject professors.

Correspondingly, faculty members have a duty to cooperate with legitimate production requests (*e.g.,* course outlines when fitness to teach is at issue) consistent with the human privilege against self-incrimination. But discovery procedures should never be used to force a faculty member to assume an ultimate burden of proof. A finding of unfitness to teach, it seems, should never be based solely on failure to produce documentary evidence.

Finally, the norms of "responsible academic procedure" which were the key element in the Inquiry Report, themselves could be somewhat modified to prevent abuse of the hearing principle. Specifically, the clause in paragraph (b) of the 1940 statement allowing written "special limitations" in classroom academic freedom in church-related schools should be eliminated. This clause is open to much abuse in church-related schools. Moreover, with the Inquiry at Catholic University, it seems to us that any legitimate interests of church sponsors can be effectively recognized as questions of professional competence and fitness to teach the religious subject matter in question. We also think that Paragraph (c) of the 1940 Statement of AAUP is not an effective statement of freedom of expression when read literally. A process of interpretation was necessary to give a workable and reasonable meaning to such words and phrases as "accuracy," "show respect," "appropriate restraint" and "make every effort." It is clear that AAUP would object to any discipline enforcing a provision of Paragraph (c) unless the violation in question was related to "fitness to teach." But the 1964 Statement on Extramural Utterance, which makes that interpretative point, and which substantially restricts the scope of Paragraph (c)'s admonitions, is technically not of the same weight of the 1940 Statement. The latter statement has been promulgated by AAUP itself, whereas the Statement on *extramural expression* is a product solely of AAUP's "Committee A" on Academic Freedom and Tenure. This technical imbalance should be eliminated. It would be perhaps timely for AAUP to consider adopting the Committee A Statement on Extramural Utterances as a formal AAUP position of equal rank with the 1940 Statement.

Furthermore, it would also seem advisable for AAUP's investigating committees seriously to reconsider the question whether the admonitions of Paragraph (c) ought even to be treated as standards enforceable in faculty dismissal proceedings. The university may well have a legitimate functional concern in preventing misuse of its name by faculty members who wrongfully purport to be official spokesmen. But other than the provision which recognizes this right, there seems to be no particular provision in Paragraph (c) which constitutes independent justification for university dismissal proceedings absent a question of fitness to teach.

A Final Consideration: We believe that the presence of attorneys during these proceedings served to clarify the real issues and to present them for analysis in a manageable form. Without question, the lawyer involved in university disciplinary proceeding must adapt himself to the particular style and method of academic inquiry. However, the academic community also must adapt in turn to the lawyer's presence and be open to the particular insights which a lawyer may be able to contribute to the workings of due process. At times in the Catholic University case, University Trustees, administrative officials and faculty members evidenced a certain hostility to the involvement of lawyers in the Inquiry and the surrounding dispute at the University. Persistent hostility to the presence of attorneys may in some circumstances effectively deny the right to counsel which AAUP rightly insists upon in university disciplinary proceedings. University faculties should be prepared both to assist counsel in their adjustment to the university forum and to guard against any resentment of the presence of counsel which might endanger the integrity of the adjudicatory process.

Notes

1. *The Advocate* (a weekly of the Archdiocese of Newark, N.J.), February 20, 1969, p. 11.

APPENDIX A

Washington, D.C. July 30, 1968

Text of Statement
by Catholic Theologians

As Roman Catholic theologians we respectfully acknowledge a distinct role of hierarchical magisterium (teaching authority) in the Church of Christ. At the same time Christian tradition assigns theologians the special responsibility of evaluating and interpreting pronouncements of the *magisterium* in the light of the total theological data operative in each question or statement. We offer these initial comments on Pope Paul VI's Encyclical on the Regulation of Birth.

The Encyclical is not an infallible teaching. History shows that a number of statements of similar or even greater authoritative weight have subsequently been proven inadequate or even erroneous. Past authoritative statements on religious liberty, interest-taking, the right to silence and the ends of marriage have all been corrected at a later date.

Many positive values concerning marriage are expressed in Paul VI's Encyclical. However, we take exception to the ecclesiology implied and the methodology used by Paul VI in the writing and promulgation of the document: they are incompatible with the Church's authentic self-awareness as expressed in and suggested by the acts of the Second Vatican Council itself. The Encyclical consistently assumes that the Church is identical with the hierarchical office. No real importance is afforded the witness of the life of the Church in its totality; the special witness of many Catholic couples is neglected; it fails to acknowledge the witness of the separated Christian Churches and Ecclesial Communities; it is insensitive to the witness of many men of good will; it pays insufficient attention to the ethical import of modern science.

Furthermore, the Encyclical betrays a narrow and positivistic notion of papal authority, as illustrated by the rejection of the majority view presented by the Commission established to consider the question, as well as by the rejection of the conclusions of a large part of the international Catholic theological community.

Likewise, we take exception to some of the specific ethical conclusions contained in the Encyclical. They are based on an inadequate concept of natural law: the multiple forms of natural law theory are ignored and the fact that competent philosophers come to different conclusions on this very question is disregarded. Even the minority report of the papal commission noted grave difficulty in attempting to present conclusive proof of the immorality of artificial contraception based on natural law.

Other defects include: overemphasis on the biological aspects of conjugal relations as ethically normative; undue stress on sexual acts and on the faculty of sex viewed in itself apart from the person and the couple; a static worldview which downplays the historical and evolutionary character of humanity in its finite existence, as described in Vatican II's *Pastoral Constitution on the Church in the Modern World;* unfounded assumptions about "the evil consequences of methods of artificial birth control"; indifference to Vatican II's assertion that prolonged sexual abstinence may cause "faithfulness to be imperiled and its quality of fruitfulness to be ruined"; an almost total disregard for the dignity of millions of human beings brought into the world without the slightest possibility of being fed and educated decently.

In actual fact, the Encyclical demonstrates no development over the teaching of Pius XI's *Casti Connubii* whose conclusions have been called into question for grave and serious reasons. These reasons, given a muffled voice at Vatican II, have not been adequately handled by the mere repetition of past teaching.

It is common teaching in the Church that Catholics may dissent from authoritative, noninfallible teachings of the magisterium when sufficient reasons for so doing exist.

Therefore, as Roman Catholic theologians, conscious of our duty and our limitations, we conclude that spouses may responsibly decide according to their conscience that artificial contraception in some circumstances is permissible and indeed necessary to preserve and foster the values and sacredness of marriage.

It is our conviction also that true commitment to the mystery of Christ and the Church requires a candid statement of mind at this time by all Catholic theologians.

APPENDIX B

News Release by Carroll A. Hochwalt, Chairman of the Board of Trustees

By unanimous vote the Board of Trustees of The Catholic University of America approved the following statement at a meeting held September 5, 1968, at the Madison Hotel in Washington, D.C.:

Statement Concerning "Dissenting Theologians" of Catholic University

The Board of Trustees of The Catholic University of America recognizes the responsibility arising from its authority to grant Pontifical degrees in sacred sciences and adheres fully to the teaching authority of the Pope speaking by his own right or together with the College of the Bishops, as set forth in the *Constitution on the Church* adopted by Vatican Council II. Further, the Board reaffirms the commitment of The Catholic University to accepted norms of academic freedom in the work of teaching and to the due process protective of such freedom.

The Board also affirms that those members of the faculty of The Catholic University who recently signed with others a statement of dissent from the teachings of the Pope in his Encyclical *Humanae Vitae* do not speak for the University. Moreover, the style and method of organizing and publicizing their dissent has raised serious questions as to the conformity of their actions with responsible academic procedure as well as with the spirit of this University.

Against this background, the Board of Trustees has unanimously reached the following conclusions:

The Board recognizes that any final judgments concerning theological teachings and any canonical decisions involving teachers of sacred sciences belong properly to the bishops of the Church. Therefore, in theological controversies this Board acknowledges the com-

206

petence and responsibility of the National Conference of Catholic Bishops and local Ordinaries.

The Board directs the acting-Rector of the University to institute through due academic process an immediate inquiry as to whether the teachers at this University who signed the recent statement of dissent have violated by their declarations or actions with respect to the Encyclical *Humanae Vitae* their responsibilities to the University under its existing statutes and under their commitments as teachers in the University and specifically as teachers of theology and/or other sacred sciences.

In order to provide for the inquiry ordered above, the Board calls for no interruption of the proper academic function of any of these faculty members who agree to abstain for the period of the inquiry from any activities which would involve the name of The Catholic University and which are inconsistent with the pronouncements of the ordinary teaching authority established in the Church—above all, that of the Holy Father.

Individual teachers unprepared to accept these conditions surrounding the inquiry are to be nonetheless assured of the continuance of their compensation but not allowed to teach during the time of the aforesaid inquiry. This alternative is established in accord with norms of the Association of American University Professors (page 43, *Academic Freedom and Tenure* A.A.U.P., 1967), which allow for the suspension of a faculty member from teaching (pending an inquiry) when his continued teaching is deemed by the governing board to be the source of possible immediate harm to others—in this instance the other members of the faculty and those several communities to which any university owes allegiance.

It is the intent of the Board of Trustees of the University by this action to protect its faculty from harm to their academic freedom and to protect the Catholic community from harm to the authentic teaching of the Church.

APPENDIX C

The Catholic University of America
Office of the Rector
Washington, D.C. 20017
December 23, 1968

Dr. Donald E. Marlowe
Dean, School of Engineering & Architecture
Catholic University

Dear Doctor Marlowe:

The Board of Trustees of The Catholic University of America is grateful to the faculty and the staff of the University for their cooperative response to the Board's statement of September 5, 1968. This resolution expressed the concern of the Board regarding the manner in which some members of the University faculty have expressed public dissent to the recent Papal Encyclical *Humanae Vitae*. The faculty committee now reviewing the style and method of this dissent has asked further clarification on the intent of the Board's directive of September 5. At the direction of the Chairman of the Board, Dr. Carroll Hochwalt, I met with a subcommittee of the Board on December 21, 1968, to prepare an answer to this question from the faculty committee.

First of all, the concern of the Board of Trustees in the current worldwide discussion of our Holy Father's Encyclical, *Humanae Vitae,* arises from the fact that this Board is ultimately responsible for the policies which guide The Catholic University of America and also responsible to Our Holy Father, Pope Paul VI, as the Supreme Teacher in the Catholic Church. The public action of certain faculty members from The Catholic University challenging the doctrine of a Papal Encyclical has caused many persons in the Church and many others to question the propriety, according to accepted academic standards, of the action of these professors. There are several publics to which the governing board of any university must account. In the current instance, many of these constituencies (including the general faculty of the University itself) have been puzzled by the manner in which some professors on the faculty of The Catholic University of America have publicly promulgated their dissent from a Papal Encyclical and have apparently undertaken to organize public opposition to this teaching. Some have expressed puzzlement not only because of the suddenness with which these actions were undertaken, but also because they seemed to some to be done without a proper regard for the person of the Holy Father and for the pastoral implications involved.

The Board of Trustees, realizing that it is accountable to these several responsible publics and also being confident of the professional competence of the faculty of the University, and being itself some distance removed from the day to day operation of the University felt the need for assistance from the teaching faculty before it could resolve in its own mind the question of how theological dissent can be expressed in the public forum with due respect for the teaching of the Holy Father and for the standards of free speculative inquiry accepted by responsible academic persons.

In the light of this dilemma, the Board on September 5, directed the acting Rector of the University to take immediate action and to delegate to a representative committee of the faculty the task of examining and reconciling, if possible, the mode in which some members of this faculty have publicly dissented from Papal teaching and the norms for expressing theological dissent which are endorsed by custom and practice among professional academic persons.

In giving this directive to the faculty of the University, the Board did not attempt to pre-judge the result of the inquiry. The Board made no charges—leveled no accusations. Furthermore, in its Statement of September 5, the Board recognized: "that any final judgments concerning theological teachings, and any canonical decisions involving teachers of sacred sciences, belong properly to the Bishops of the Church.

Therefore, in theological controversies, this Board acknowledges the competence and responsibility of the National Conference of Catholic Bishops and local Ordinaries."

Hence, the focus of the present inquiry is on the style and method whereby some faculty members expressed personal dissent from Papal teaching, and apparently helped organize additional public dissent to such teaching. At no time in this inquiry is there any attempt by the Board to question the right of a scholar to have or to hold private dissent on Papal teaching not defined as infallible.

There is a considerable body of commentary on the method and spirit of due dissent in the Catholic Theological community. However, the literature now available in the general academic community on how believing Christians reconcile the tenets of their religious faith with the demands of authentic speculative investigation is almost non-existent. Witness the best statements in print from the AAUP and the Association of American Theological Schools on this subject. As one searches these professional sources for guidance, one quickly realizes that many concerned persons far beyond the campus of The Catholic University of America are eager to have in print statements which are both academically and theologically respectable on the proper balance for teaching and writing in the sacred sciences.

It is possible that the current inquiry could result in an historic statement for the entire field of speculative theology. We are confident that this fact is appreciated by the members of our faculty conducting the current review of this general question and the particular question of its application here and now.

It is the mind of the Board of Trustees that the inquiry now in progress will review the standards of responsible faculty procedure endorsed by American universities in matters of public debate or controversy. Do such standards exist? If so, how does one show that the procedures of our faculty in the current matter follow or depart from such norms? These are questions the Board poses to the faculty committee.

The Board further asks the faculty inquiry committee whether it finds any discrepancy between the mode of public dissent followed by some members of The Catholic University of America faculty, and the obligations accepted by these professors as members of the University faculty. The terms of their employment, the statutes of the University, and the profession of Catholic Faith made by these professors would seem to be some of the sources to be consulted by the faculty in arriving at their answer to this question.

The Board of Trustees in its Statement of September 5 made no prejudgments on the facts or the standards. The Statement is not an accusation; it is a request for the widest possible faculty participation in determining how this faculty, this Board, this University can best accomplish, in the present instance and for the future, their common tasks of advancing authentic intellectual investigation and of demonstrating in action their promise of fidelity to the teachings of the Catholic Church.

In the final paragraphs of its Statement, the Board endeavored to create a climate within which the current review could be conducted with charity, clarity and out of the heat of controversy. The Board is appreciative of the ready and gracious acceptance of these conditions by the faculty members concerned.

Sincerely yours,

Brother Nivard Scheel, c.f.x.
Acting Rector

APPENDIX D

Academic Senate

Committee B

October 16, 1968

Procedures for the Conduct of the Inquiry Directed by the Board of Trustees into the Declarations and Actions of Certain Members of the Faculty of the Catholic University of America:

1. *Membership of the Board of Inquiry*
The Board of Inquiry shall consist of five persons. These persons shall be elected by the elected faculty representatives of the Academic Senate. One Board member shall be elected from each of the three main divisions of the faculty of the University, i.e., the Graduate School of Arts and Sciences, the Professional School and the Ecclesiastical Schools. The other two members shall be elected at large without regard to their parent faculty but rather with regard to their capability to serve. In particular, one of the members elected at large should be from outside the University and competent in the sacred sciences.

In carrying out this election, the elected Senate members from a particular division shall act as a nominating committee for the single candidacy assigned to their division.* The Senate Committee on Committees and Rules shall act as a nominating committee to propose names for the two candidates to be elected at large. In addition, the Committee shall nominate and the elected members of the Senate shall elect a member of the faculty of the University as an alternate member

*To avoid a potential conflict of interest, the School of Theology should elect, in the place of its current delegate, another member of the faculty of the School of Theology, who is not a party, to serve in his stead on the nominating committee.

of the Board to sit with the Board during the course of the Inquiry, and to serve as a member in case of any vacancy on the Board.

2. *Board Chairman*

The Board members shall elect from among themselves their own chairman who shall be a member of the University faculty but not from the faculty of any of the Ecclesiastical Schools.

3. *Scope of Inquiry: Powers of Board*

a) The scope of the Inquiry shall be to determine whether the faculty members ". . . who signed the recent statement of dissent have violated by their declarations or actions with respect to the encyclical *Humanae Vitae* their responsibilities to the University under its existing statutes and under their commitments as teachers in the University and specifically as teachers of theology and/or other sacred sciences. . ." and whether under "accepted norms of academic freedom" their actions have conformed "with responsible academic procedure as well as with the spirit of this University."

b) The Board shall receive all evidence, documents and testimony relevant to the Inquiry, seek out and invite appropriate witnesses, and formulate from the testimony and evidence produced conclusions and recommendations for transmission to the Rector and Board of Trustees.

In exercising the above the Board may give due attention and consideration to differing conduct and circumstances of individual parties and may reflect such individual differences and distinctions in its conclusions and recommendations.

4. *Powers of Chairman of the Board of Inquiry*

As used herein, the term "Chairman" includes any member of the Board presiding in the absence of the elected Chairman.

The Chairman of the Board of Inquiry shall act for the Board, and shall have the following powers:

a) To open, continue or adjourn the Inquiry;

b) To determine the admissibility of and to receive evidence and to regulate the course of the Inquiry;

c) To dispose of procedural requests or similar matters;

d) To take any other action necessary or incident to the orderly conduct of the Inquiry.

5. *Parties to the Inquiry*

a) The parties to the Inquiry shall consist of those persons described in the September 5, 1968, statement of the Board of Trustees, and designated as faculty members by the Rector on 21 October 1968; and such additional persons designated by the Rector as will assure complete and thorough amplification of the issues before the Board.

b) Each party is entitled:

  i) to be informed in advance of the procedures to be followed by the Board of Inquiry;

 ii) to receive adequate notice of, and to attend, all proceedings of the Board of Inquiry other than its own deliberations;

iii) to select and call witnesses, including witnesses specially qualified in the fields of competence related to the Inquiry;

 iv) to have the assistance of the Board of Inquiry or the Technical Staff, when necessary, in securing the attendance or written testimony of witnesses and the production of pertinent documentary evidence;

  v) to be informed of the identity of those witnesses whose statements of necessity are taken outside of the Inquiry, and of the contents of such statements; and

 vi) to be represented at all stages by counsel of his choosing.

6. *Observers*

The Board of Inquiry may designate or invite as observers representatives from the Board of Trustees, from the University Administration, from the University's Assembly of Professors, from the American Association of University Professors, and from the student body. Such observers are entitled to receive notice of, and to attend, all proceedings of the Board of Inquiry other than its own deliberations and the pre-Inquiry conference.

7. *Technical Staff*

The Board of Inquiry, after consultation with all parties, shall designate a Technical Staff from within or without the University to assist it in determining appropriate witnesses, in receiving evidence and documents, in examining witnesses, and in determining the relevancy, materiality, and competency of evidence.

8. *Pre-Inquiry Conference*
The Chairman of the Board of Inquiry shall hold a pre-Inquiry conference with the parties to the Inquiry and the Technical Staff at a convenient time and place prior to the Inquiry. At such conference the Chairman shall exchange with the parties the names and number of witnesses to be called at the Inquiry, the areas in which they will be examined and the exhibits which will be offered in evidence. The Chairman shall also determine with the parties the extent to which written statements will be accepted from witnesses in lieu of testimony, the limits (if any) on the number of witnesses or exhibits, the order in which testimony will be presented, and general arrangements for the conduct of the Inquiry.

9. *Examination of witnesses*
a) Witnesses will be examined by members of the Board of Inquiry, or, upon delegation, by the Technical Staff. Following such examination, the parties to the Inquiry will be given an opportunity to examine such witnesses.

b) Materiality, relevancy and competency of witnesses' testimony, exhibits or other evidence will not be the subject of objections by a party or any other person, but such matters will be controlled by rulings of the Chairman on his own motion. If the examination of a witness by a party is interrupted by a ruling of the Chairman, opportunity will be given to show materiality, relevancy or competency of the testimony or evidence sought to be produced.

10. *Evidence*
The Chairman shall receive all testimony and evidence which might be of aid to the Board in discharging its duties. He may waive limitations imposed at the pre-Inquiry conference, and may exclude any testimony or exhibits which are not pertinent to the Inquiry or which are merely redundant or otherwise not in order.

11. *Recommendations by parties*
Any party may submit to the Board his recommendations (and reasons

therefor) as to the proper conclusions to be drawn from the testimony and evidence submitted at the Inquiry.

12. *Stenographic transcript*
A verbatim report of the Inquiry shall be taken, and shall remain in the custody of the Chairman until the Board of Inquiry is discharged. When transcribed, the transcript shall be available to the parties.

13. *Private nature of the Inquiry*
Neither the proceedings of the Board of Inquiry, nor the record therein, shall be open to the public, the press, or the University community. The Chairman may from time to time determine with the parties to issue announcements relating to the time and place of meetings of the Board and the general progress of the Inquiry.

14. *Disclosure of record of the Inquiry*
The record of the Inquiry shall consist of the transcript, exhibits and documents submitted in the course of the Inquiry, and the written conclusions and recommendations of the Board. Upon completion of the Inquiry, the record shall be disclosed to the Academic Senate, the Rector and the parties. The Academic Senate shall disclose the record of the Inquiry to the public at an appropriate time after its report to the Rector, provided that the Senate may withhold from public disclosure any portions of the record which it seems to be detrimental to the reputation or well-being of any party or the University community.

15. *Expenses*
The University shall bear the expense of supplying to the parties copies, in reasonable quantity, of transcripts and documentary evidence, of necessary translations, and of travel and related disbursements of specially qualified witnesses called by them, other than such specially qualified witnesses whose testimony the Board may deem adequately presentable in written form.

The University shall also bear the expense of supplying to the Board any necessary supplies and equipment, and an appropriate research and secretarial staff.

16. *Modification of Rules*
These rules of procedure may be varied, modified or waived by the
joint agreement of all parties and the members of the Board of Inquiry.

Committee B Members
Dr. Donald E. Marlowe, Chairman
Reverend James Coriden
Dean Ralph Rahner
Dr. Frank A. Andrews
Dr. Maxwell Bloomfield

Index

AAC See: Association of American Colleges

AATS See: American Association of Theological Schools; *1960 Statement,* AATS

AATS Statement See: *1960 Statement,* AATS

AAU See: American Association of Universities

AAUP See: American Association of University Professors

Academic Senate, Catholic University 13,33,36,37,45,46,150,152, 163,169–172,184; June 4 Meeting 169; June 5 Resolutions 170,172 See also: Academic Senate, Procedure for the Inquiry; Committees A & B, Academic Senate

Academic Senate, Procedure for the Inquiry 36,37,45,198,199 Text: 212–217 See also: Academic Senate, June 4 Meeting 169 and June 5 Resolutions 170,172

ACLU See: American Civil Liberties Union

ACLU Statement 77,78 See also: American Civil Liberties Union

Advisory Letter No. 11 71,73

Alabama Polytechnic Institute case 68–70,73,74,83

Alfrink, Bernard 40

American Association of Theological Schools 86,94–97,125,127,130 135,138,161,162 See also: *1960 Statement,* AATS

American Association of Universities 52,57,75,76,161 See also: *1953 Statement,* AAU

American Association of University Professors 16,28–30,33–35,43,61, 65–73,75–83,86–97,99,100,102, 122,123,125,127,130,138–141, 146–148,150,152,160,166,168, 181,183,190,193–195,198–201 See also: *Declaration by the Committee on Academic Freedom and Tenure;* Committee A of AAUP; Special Committee on Academic Freedom in Church-Related Institutions, 1965; *1940 Statement,* AAUP; *1958 Statement,* AAUP; *1964 Statement,* Committee A of AAUP; *1966 Statement,* AAUP

American bishops 3,5,7,9,31,39,137, 143,145,179,184,193 See also: National Conference of Catholic Bishops; *Church In Our Day; Human Life In Our Day; Whalen's Special Communication*

American Civil Liberties Union 29, 77,78,161 See also: *ACLU Statement*

Apostles Creed 108

Apostolic delegate See: Raimondi, Luigi

218